JN075266

フィンランド式
小学英語
ワークブック
初 級

米崎 里・岩﨑幸子・川見和子

清風堂書店

はじめに

こんにちは、みなさん！

このワークブックは、みなさんが英語を勉強するときのお手伝いとなるように、北欧のフィンランドの小学校で使われている英語ワークブックを参考にして作りました。

「なぜフィンランド?」と思うかもしれませんが、フィンランドの小学校で使われている英語ワークブックは、たくさん役立つエクササイズ（練習）やアクティビティ（活動）が提供されています。そしてそのエクササイズやアクティビティは、楽しく学べるよう工夫されており、何よりも、**英語の力が着実に向上します**。そんなワークブックが日本にもあればなあと思い、日本の小学生向けにフィンランド式の英語ワークブックを開発しました。

このフィンランド式の英語ワークブックは、教室ではもちろんのこと、**自宅でも一人で楽しく勉強できるように工夫されている**ので、**自然と学習する習慣が身につき**、英語を勉強するのがもっと楽しくなります。

このワークブックを実際使ってくれた奈良市の公立小学校の子どもたちから次のような声が届きました。

- ゲームをするような感覚で英語ができ、楽しく学べた。

- 最初はぶあついと思ったけど、イラストとかがたくさんあって、無理なくできた。

- 英語のワークブックのおかげで英語ができるようになった。

- 難しいところもあったけど、すべてできて満足。もっと英語力を高めたい。

このワークブックの特長は、次のとおりです。

1. 学校で習ったことをもう一度くりかえし学べます。
2. **豊富なイラストを通して英語を理解**できます。
3. **楽しく、ゲーム感覚**で学べます。
4. 単語や表現をくりかえし学べるため、**自然に英語を覚える**ことができます。
5. 家や学校で、**一人で学習できる**ようになっています。
6. **英語を「使う」ことを目的**としたエクササイズやアクティビティを行うことで、**暗記だけに頼らずに英語の力をつける**ことができます。

さあ、いっしょにフィンランド式の英語ワークブックで楽しく学びながら、英語を身につけましょう！

本書の使い方

本書は学校で学んだことを、一人でも学べる家庭学習用のワークブックです。UNIT（ユニット）の展開はおよそ次のようになっています。

①Target Sentences（ターゲットセンテンス）

UNIT で学ぶ目標文が示されています。QR コードで音声を聞くことができます。英語の意味を日本語で確認（かくにん）します。

②新出単語

UNIT5（p.27）から新出単語とその意味が表示されています。QR コードで音声を聞き、自信を持って英語で言えるまで何度もくり返し練習します。

③単語に関する Exercise（エクササイズ）

新出単語に関する複数のエクササイズ（ふくすう）を準備（じゅんび）しています。まずはしっかりと単語を定着させます。例えば UNIT5 でいうと、2 (p.27) や 3 (p.28)の問題になります。

④表現（文法）に関する Exercise（エクササイズ）

学習する表現（文法）に関するエクササイズを複数準備（ふくすうじゅんび）しています。例えば UNIT5 でいうと、8 (p.29) や 9 (p.30)の問題になります。先に学んだ単語を使っていますので、単語の復習もできます。

⑤Chants（チャンツ）

チャンツは、リズムのある簡単な表現や文をくりかえして練習する活動です。UNIT で学習した単語や表現を使いチャンツを作っています。QR コードで音声が流れますので、英語のリズムを楽しめます。例えば UNIT5 でいえば、10 (p.30)の問題になります。

⑥ Key Points（キーポイント）

UNIT で学習する目標文を日本語と英語でまとめています。

⑦統合的な Activity（アクティビティ） （とうごうてき）

UNIT で学習した単語や表現（文法）を使い、英語を使うことを目的としたアクティビティです。例えば、UNIT5 でいうと、12 (p.32)の問題になります。

⑧EXTRA(エクストラ)

2つから4つの UNIT の学習を終えた後、これまで学習した単語や表現をもう一度学べる復習ページとなっています。

> なお、日本の教科書などでは「a」「g」「t」という表記に統一されていますが、フィンランドのワークブックでは様々な書体を使用して遊び心を出しているため、本書では「a」「g」「t」という表記も使用しています。

もくじ

2

UNIT 1

Target Sentences

Who are you?	あなたはだれですか？
- I'm Emily.	- わたしはエミリーです。
What's your name?	あなたの名前は何ですか。
- My name is Jack.	- ぼくの名前はジャックです。
Jack is my friend.	ジャックは私の友達です。

大問1

1 よく聞いて、くりかえし言おう。

Good morning.   Good afternoon.   Good night.

大問2

2 聞こえてきた順番を数字で書こう。

(   )   (   )   (   )

3 英語と日本語を結ぼう。

1. Good morning.   ・   ・おやすみなさい。
2. Good afternoon.   ・   ・おはようございます。
3. Goodbye.   ・   ・やあ。
4. Hello.   ・   ・こんにちは（午後のあいさつ）。
5. Good night.   ・   ・さようなら。

4 よく聞いて、くりかえし言おう。

Good morning, everybody.
みなさん

Good morning, Ms. Brown.

Goodbye, class.
クラスのみなさん

Goodbye, Mr. Green.

5 先生のあいさつを聞いて、答えよう。

1. Ms. Brown　　　2. Mr. Green　　　3. Mr. / Ms. ＿＿＿＿＿＿＿

あなたの先生の名前

6 よく聞いて、くりかえし言おう。

Emily　　　　Jack　　　　Alice　　　　Fred

＿＿＿＿にイラストの人物の名前を入れて言おう。

1. Hello!　I'm ＿＿＿＿ .

2. My name is ＿＿＿＿ .

3. Hi!　I'm ＿＿＿＿ .

4. Hello!　My name is ＿＿＿＿ .

4

7 英語を聞きながら、○をつけよう。

大問7

goodbye morningnighthello

8 日本語の意味にあう方に、○をつけよう。

1. (my / your) name 　　あなたの名前

2. (my / your) friend 　　私の友達

3. (my / your) teacher 　　私の先生

4. (my / your) classmate 　　あなたのクラスメート

大問9

9 よく聞いて、くりかえし言おう。

Who are you?

I'm Emily.
What's your name?

My name is Jack.

10 ＿＿＿＿に英語を入れて、Emilyと会話をしよう。

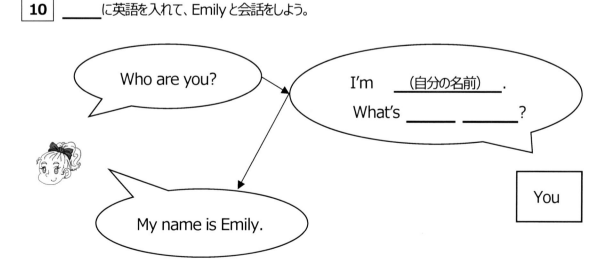

Who are you?

I'm ＿＿(自分の名前)＿＿.
What's ＿＿＿ ＿＿＿?

My name is Emily.

You

5

Key Points 英語、日本語の順に声に出して読もう。

I　わたしは	you　あなたは
my　　わたしの	your　あなたの
I am Fred. わたしはフレッドです。	You are my classmate. あなたはわたしのクラスメートです。
My teacher is Mr. Green. わたしの先生はグリーン先生です。	Your teacher is Ms. Brown. あなたの先生はブラウン先生です。
Who are you? あなたはだれですか。	I'm… . わたしは…です。
What's your name? あなたの名前は何ですか。	My name is… . わたしの名前は…です。

11 よく聞いて、読まれた方に○をつけよう。

大問6

例)　I　(am) / are　　Jane.

1.　Emily　is / are　my 友^{とも}だ^だち^ち friend.

2.　What's　your / you　name?

3.　Who are　your / you　?

4.　I / My　am Fred.

5.　Mr. Green is　you / my　teacher.

12 英語をなぞろう。

Hello.

Good morning.

Goodbye.

What's your name?

My name is Kenta.

13 ____に英語を入れ言おう。

1. What's _____ name?   あなたの

2. _____ name is Miho.   わたしの

3. Who are _____?   あなたは

4. _____ your teacher.   (わたしは)～です

I'm

My

are

you

your

UNIT 2

Target Sentences

> Where are you from? あなたはどこの出身ですか。
>
> - I'm from Japan. - わたしは日本の出身です。

1 よく聞いて、くりかえし言おう。

大問1

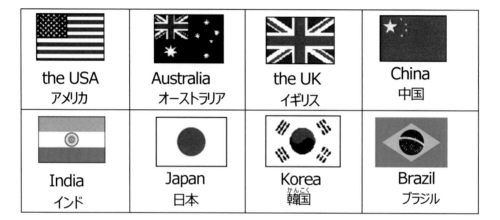

the USA アメリカ	Australia オーストラリア	the UK イギリス	China 中国
India インド	Japan 日本	Korea かんこく 韓国	Brazil ブラジル

大問2

2 聞こえてきた順番を数字で書こう。

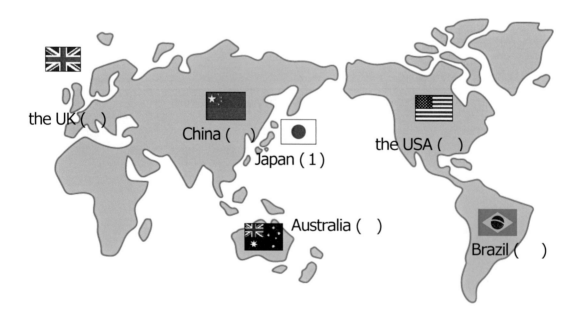

the UK（　）

China（　）

Japan（１）

the USA（　）

Australia（　）

Brazil（　）

8

3 例にならって、国旗にあうようにアルファベットを結びつけよう。

1. 　🇰🇷　　Ko　・　　　　・ tralia

2. 　🇦🇺　　Aus　・　　　　・ zil

3. 　🇯🇵　　Ja　・　　　　・ dia

4. 　🇮🇳　　In　・　　　　・ pan

5. 　🇧🇷　　Bra　・　　　　・ rea

4 よく聞いて、くりかえし言おう。

1. **Where are you from?**　－ I'm from Japan.

2. **Where are you from?**　－ I'm from Australia.

3. **Where are you from?**　－ I'm from Brazil.

4. **Where are you from ?**　－ I'm from the UK.

5. **Where are you from ?**　－ I'm from the USA.

6. **Where are you from ?**　－ I'm from Korea.

9

5 よく聞いて、くりかえし言おう。

Where are you from?
I'm from the UK.

Where are you from?
I'm from Brazil.

I'm from Japan.
はじめまして
Nice to meet you!

Nice to meet you, too!

6 よく聞いて、それぞれの出身地に〇をつけよう。

国 ＼ 名前	1. Emily	2. Jack	3. Ana	4. Lin
China 				
the UK				
Brazil				
the USA	〇			
Australia				

Key Points 英語、日本語の順に声に出して読もう。

Where are you from?	I'm from…
あなたはどこの出身ですか。	わたしは・・・の出身です。
	I'm from Brazil.
	わたしはブラジルの出身です。

10

7 ＿＿＿の国を自由にかえて言おう。

> Where are you from?

> I'm from <u>the UK</u>.

the USA

India

Korea

Brazil

China

Australia

大問8(1)

8 よく聞いて、次の会話を練習しよう。

1回目 音声の後に続いて言おう。

大問8(2)

2回目 Emily のパートを言おう

3回目 Jack のパートを言おう。

大問8(3)

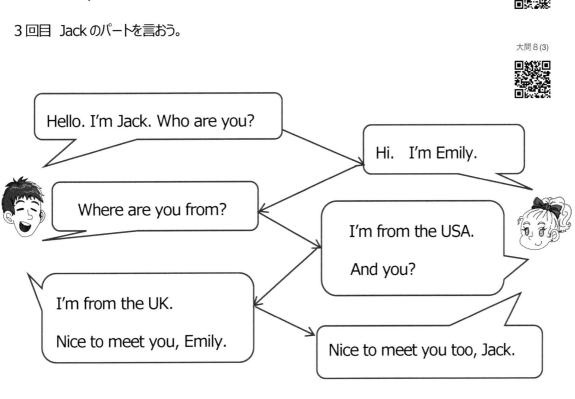

> Hello. I'm Jack. Who are you?

> Hi. I'm Emily.

> Where are you from?

> I'm from the USA.
> And you?

> I'm from the UK.
> Nice to meet you, Emily.

> Nice to meet you too, Jack.

11

UNIT 3

Target Sentences

How old are you?　　あなたは何才ですか。

- I'm eleven　　－　１１才です。

- I'm elven, too.　　－　わたしも１１才です。

大問1

1 よく聞いて、くりかえし言おう。

| 1 | 2 | 3 | 4 | 5 |
| one | two | three | four | five |

| 6 | 7 | 8 | 9 | 10 |
| six | seven | eight | nine | ten |

| 11 | 12 |
| eleven | twelve |

大問2

2 聞こえた数字を書こう。

1.　[　　　] → [　　] → [　　　] → [　　　]

2.　[　　　] → [　　] → [　　　] → [　　　]

3.　[　　　] → [　　] → [　　　] → [　　　]

3 例にならって、数字を書こう。

two___2___   six_____   three_____   eleven_____   eight_____

twelve_____   four_____   nine_____   five_____   seven_____

4 1～12まで順につなごう。

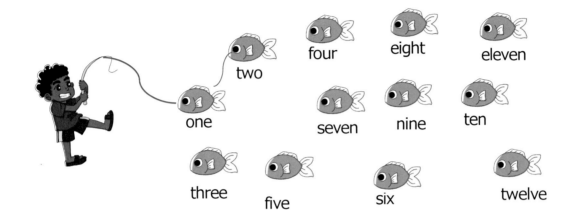

5 絵を見て、いくつあるか数字を選んで言おう。

four

five

six

seven

eight

nine

ten

eleven

_____ cakes   _____ doughnuts   _____ cherries

6 例にならって、計算した答えを数字で書いて、英語で言おう。

one + one = 2

1. one + two = _____

2. three + four = _____

3. four + five = _____

4. seven + one = _____

5. three – two = _____

6. five – one = _____

7. eight – two = _____

8. twelve – two = _____

7 絵を見て数を英語で書こう。水色のます目を上から読んで、出てきた数字を英語で書こう。

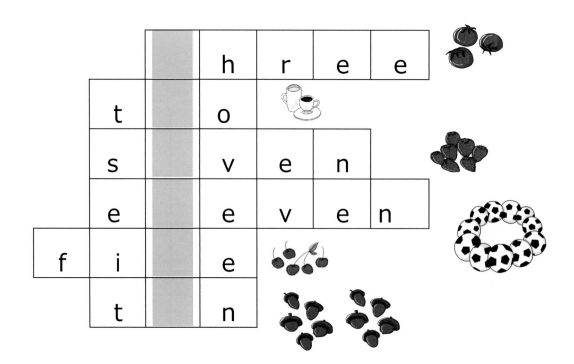

出てきた数字

_____

14

8 よく聞いて、くりかえし言おう。

大問8

How old are you?

Eleven or ten?

I'm eleven, not ten.

How old are you?

Eleven or ten?

I'm eleven too, not ten.

Ten   Eleven

eleven

ten   ten

Ten

eleven

Eleven

大問9

9 会話を聞いて、4人の年令(ねんれい)を数字で書こう。

Kenta	Ana	Jack	Lucy

Key Points 英語、日本語の順に声に出して読もう。

How old…?	I'm….
何才ですか…？	わたしは…才です。
	I'm ten.
	わたしは１０才です。

15

10 よく聞いて、次の会話を練習しよう。

大問10(1) 大問10(2) 大問10(3)

1回目　音声の後に続いて言おう。
2回目　Fred のパートを言おう。
3回目　Emily のパートを言おう。

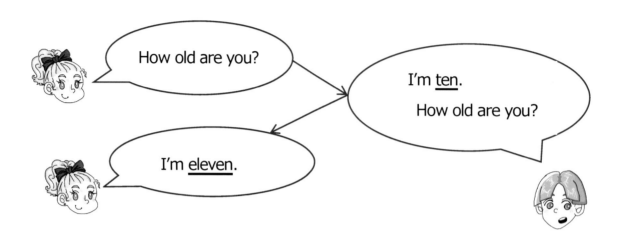

How old are you?

I'm <u>ten</u>.
How old are you?

I'm <u>eleven</u>.

11 英語をなぞろう。

How old are you?

I'm eleven.

12 日本語にあうように＿＿＿に英語を入れて言おう。

1. ＿＿＿＿＿ ＿＿＿＿＿ **are you?**　　　あなたは何才ですか。

2. ＿＿＿＿＿ **eleven.**　　　　　　　わたしは 11 才です。

I'm

How

old

16

UNIT 4

Target Sentences

I'm hungry.	わたしはおなかがすいています。
I'm not hungry.	わたしはおなかがすいていません。
You're tired.	あなたはつかれています。
You're not tired.	あなたはつかれていません。
Are you sleepy?	あなたはねむいですか。
- Yes, I am.	－ はい、ねむいです。
- No, I'm not.	－ いいえ、ねむくありません。

大問1

1 よく聞いて、くりかえし言おう。

happy	hungry	sleepy	tired	fine
うれしい	おなかがすいた	ねむい	つかれた	元気な

大問2

2 聞こえてきた順に番号をつけよう。

うれしい	元気な	おなかがすいた	つかれた	ねむい
＿＿	＿＿	＿＿	＿＿	＿＿

17

3 よく聞いて、くりかえし言おう。

4 下から文を選んで、not の文にして言おう。

例)　I'm hungry.　→　I'm **not** hungry.

　　You're happy.　→　You're **not** happy.

5 よく聞いて、くりかえし言おう。

I'm happy.
I'm not angry.
<small>おこっている</small>

I'm thirsty.
<small>のどがかわいて</small>

I'm not hungry.

I'm tired.
But I'm OK.
<small>でもだいじょうぶ</small>

I'm not No.1.
But I'm great!
<small>すばらしい</small>

6 よく聞いて、くりかえし言おう。

Are you <u>tired</u>?

Yes, I am.

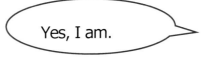

No, I'm not.

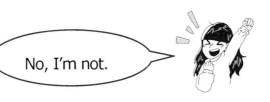

7 よく聞いて、それぞれの質問に Yes, I am. か No, I'm not. で答えよう。
<small>しつもん</small>

1. Are you fine?

2. Are you sleepy?

3. Are you happy?

4. Are you hungry?

5. Are you tired?

Yes, I am.

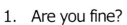
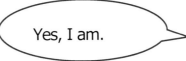

No, I'm not.

19

Key Points 英語、日本語の順に声に出して読もう。

I'm…. = I am…. わたしは・・・です。	You're…. = You are…. あなたは・・・です。
I'm not …. = I am not…. わたしは・・・ではありません。	You're not [You aren't] …. = You are not…. あなたは・・・ではありません。
I'm not twelve. わたしは１２才ではありません。	You're not [You aren't] twelve. あなたは１２才ではありません。
	Are you…? あなたは・・・ですか。

	Are you hungry?
	 あなたはおなかがすいていますか。
	 - Yes, I am.
	  - はい、すいています。
	 - No, I'm not.
	  - いいえ、すいていません。

---

8 例にならって、質問と答えを選ぼう。

1. Are you from the UK ?　　・　　・ No, I'm not. I'm not sleepy.

2. Are you happy?　　・　　・ Yes, I am. I'm hungry.

3 Are you sleepy?　　・　　・ No, I'm not. I'm eleven.

4. Are you hungry?　　・　　・ Yes, I am. I'm happy.

5. Are you twelve?　　・　　・ No, I'm not. I'm from the USA.

20

9 英語をなぞろう。

I'm not sleepy.

You're not eleven.

Are you from the USA?

- Yes, I am.

- No, I'm not.

10 例にならって、_____ に英語を入れて言おう。

例) **I'm not hungry.**　　　わたしはおなかがすいていません。
　　You're not tired.　　　あなたはつかれていません。

1. **I'm** _____ **sleepy.**　　　わたしはねむくありません。

2. _____ _____ **twelve.**　　　わたしは１２才ではありません。

3. **You're** _____ **from Brazil.**　　　あなたはブラジルの出身ではありません。

4. _____ _____ **eleven.**　　　あなたは１１才ではありません。

 You're　　 I'm　　 not

11 例にならって、___ に英語を入れて言おう。

例) <u>Are</u> you hungry ?　　　　　あなたはおなかがすいていますか。

　　- Yes, <u>I</u> am.　　　　　　　　- はい、すいています。

　　- No, I'm <u>not</u>.　　　　　　　- いいえ、すいていません。

1. _____ you tired?　　　あなたはつかれていますか。

　　- No, I'm _____　　　　- いいえ、つかれていません。

2. Are _____ from the USA?　　あなたはアメリカの出身ですか。

　　- Yes, I _____　　　　　　- はい、そうです。

EXTRA (UNIT 1 – UNIT 4)

1 英語を聞いて、それに返事しよう。

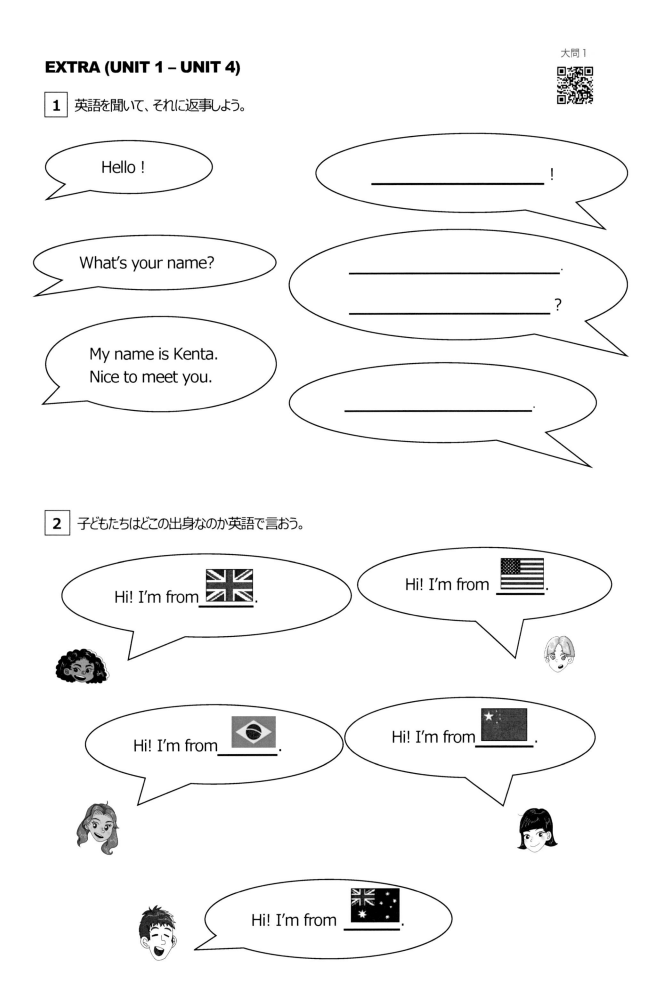

Hello !

_____ !

What's your name?

_____ .

_____ ?

My name is Kenta.
Nice to meet you.

_____ .

2 子どもたちはどこの出身なのか英語で言おう。

Hi! I'm from _____ .

Hi! I'm from _____ .

Hi! I'm from _____ .

Hi! I'm from _____ .

Hi! I'm from _____ .

3 英語を聞いて、単語と国旗を結ぼう。

1. Japan　　2. the UK　　3. Brazil　　4. China　　5. Korea　　6. India

　・　　　　・　　　　・　　　　・　　　　・　　　　・

　・　　　　・　　　　・　　　　・　　　　・　　　　・

4 下の英語をイラストで表そう。

1.

2.

3.

sleepy　　　　　happy　　　　　hungry

5 イラストにあうように線で結ぼう。

1. **h a p** ・　　　　・ **y**

2. **h u n g** ・　　　　・ **l e v e n**

3. **s l e e p** ・　　　　・ **r y**

4. **s e v** ・　　　　・ **p y**

5. **e** ・　　　　・ **e n**

24

6 例にならって、英語の質問を聞いて、答えを選び、言おう。

1. Who are you ?　·

2. 元気ですか
How are you ?　·

3. Are you hungry?　·　·

4. How old are you ?　·　·

· I'm fine. Thank you.

· I'm Kenta.

I'm eleven.

No. I'm not

7 例にならって、正しい順番になるよう（　）に番号を入れよう。

例) are － how － you －?
　　（2）　（1）　（3）

1. you － Are － hungry －?
　　（　）　（　）　（　）

2. are － from － you － Where －?
　　（　）　（　）　（　）　（　）

3. you － from － Are － Korea －?
　　（　）　（　）　（　）　（　）

25

8 例にならって、名前を選びその人になりきって自己しょうかいをしよう。

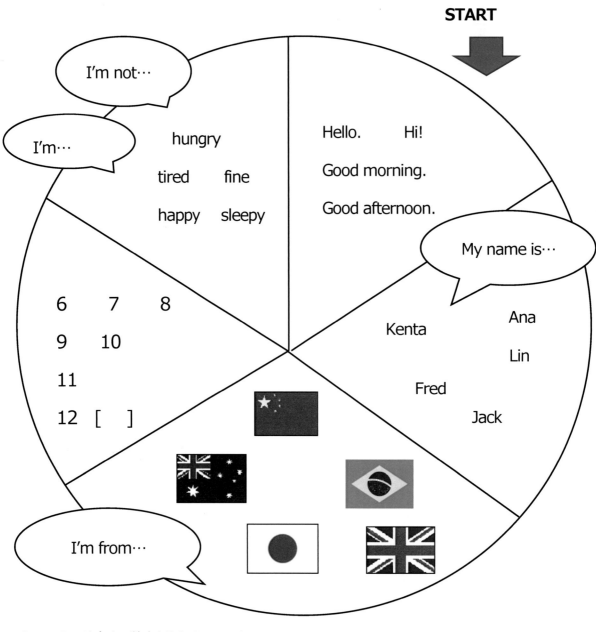

[   ] には自由に数字を入れよう。

例) **Hi!   My name is Kenta.   I'm from Japan.   I'm eleven.**
I'm fine.   I'm not hungry.   Nice to meet you!

UNIT 5

Target Sentences

I like red.	私は赤色が好きです。		
I don't like math.	私は算数が好きではありません。		
Do you like blue?	あなたは青色が好きですか。		
- Yes, I do.	– はい、好きです。		
Do you like science?	あなたは理科が好きですか。		
- No, I don't.	– いいえ、好きではありません。		

大問1

1 よく聞いて、くりかえし言おう。

red	赤	●	science	理科
blue	青	●	math	算数
green	緑	●	Japanese	国語
black	黒	●	English	英語
white	白	○	social studies	社会
orange	オレンジ	●	P.E.	体育
pink	ピンク	●	music	音楽

大問2

2 聞こえてきた順番を数字で書こう。

1. 緑（　　　）　　赤（　　　）　　オレンジ（　　　）　　青（　　　）

2. 青（　　　）　　白（　　　）　　黒（　　　）　　ピンク（　　　）

27

3 英語と日本語を結ぼう。

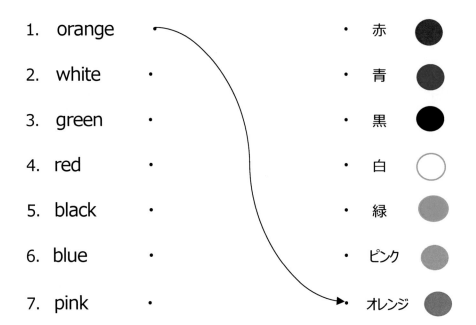

1. orange   ・

2. white   ・

3. green   ・

4. red   ・

5. black   ・

6. blue   ・

7. pink   ・

・ 赤

・ 青

・ 黒

・ 白

・ 緑

・ ピンク

・ オレンジ

4 red のあとに black をふくめ、6つ色の単語が続いています。単語を見つけて○で囲もう。

redbluepinkgreenblackorangewhite

5 聞こえてきた方に○をつけよう。

大問5

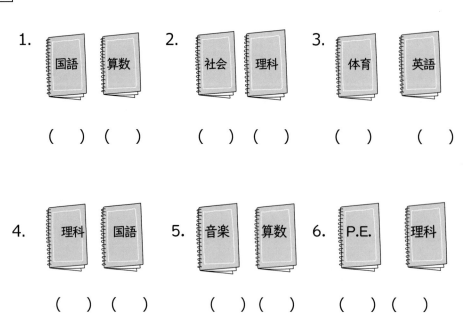

1. 国語 算数   2. 社会 理科   3. 体育 英語

( ) ( )   ( ) ( )   ( )   ( )

4. 理科 国語   5. 音楽 算数   6. P.E. 理科

( ) ( )   ( ) ( )   ( ) ( )

6 聞こえてきた順番を数字で書こう。

1.

国語 ( ) 　算数 ( ) 　社会 ( ) 　音楽 ( ) 　理科 ( )

2.

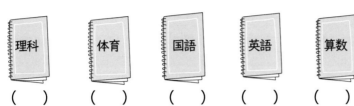

理科 ( ) 　体育 ( ) 　国語 ( ) 　英語 ( ) 　算数 ( )

7 ＿＿＿＿＿＿に日本語の教科名を書こう。

1. science ＿＿＿＿＿

2. music ＿＿＿＿＿

3. English ＿＿＿＿＿

4. Japanese ＿＿＿＿＿

5. social studies ＿＿＿＿＿

6. math ＿＿＿＿＿

7. P.E. ＿＿＿＿＿

> 国語　算数　理科　社会　体育　英語　音楽

8 よく聞いて、くりかえし言おう。

> I like orange.
> （私はオレンジ色が好きです）

> I **don't** like orange.
> （私はオレンジ色が好きではありません）

1. I like blue. 　　　　　I **don't** like blue.

2. I like science. 　　　　I **don't** like science.

3. I like P.E. 　　　　　I **don't** like P.E.

4. I like math. 　　　　　I **don't** like math.

9 よく聞いて、質問に対する自分の答えを言おう。

1. Do you like *tempura*?   - Yes, I do.   /   No, I don't.

2. Do you like *ramen*?   - Yes, I do.   /   No, I don't.

3. Do you like *sukiyaki*?   - Yes, I do.   /   No, I don't.

4. Do you like *sushi*?   - Yes, I do.   /   No, I don't.

5. Do you like *takoyaki*?   - Yes, I do.   /   No, I don't.

6. Do you like *tofu*?   - Yes, I do.   /   No, I don't.

10 よく聞いて、くりかえし言おう。

Do you like blue?
   Yes, I do.
   I like the blue sky^空.

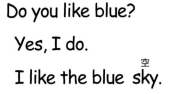

Do you like red?
   Yes, I do.
   I like red tulips^{チューリップ}.

Do you like white?
   Yes, I do.
   I like white snow^雪.

Do you like orange?
   Yes, I do.
   I like orange oranges!

30

Key Points 英語、日本語の順に声に出して読もう。

I like …	I don't like …	Do you like … ?
わたしは…が好きです。	わたしは…が好きではありません。	あなたは…が好きですか。
I like Japanese. わたしは国語が好きです。	I don't like red. わたしは赤色が好きではありません。	Do you like science? あなたは理科が好きですか。 Yes, I do. - はい、好きです。 No, I don't. - いいえ、好きではありません。

11 例にならって、Jack, Emily, Alice の英語が答えとなる質問を作ろう。

例)

Do you like science?　Yes, I do. I like science.

Do you like math?　No, I don't. I don't like math.

1. 　Yes, I do. I like social studies.

2. 　No, I don't. I don't like P.E.

3. 　No, I don't. I don't like music.

31

12 サイコロの目の数だけ進んだら、その食べ物や色や教科が好きかどうか言おう。何度かくりかえしてみよう。

I like *sushi*.

I don't like blue.

13 英語をなぞろう。

I like black.

I don't like green.

Do you like math?

– Yes, I do.

14 日本語にあうように、_____に英語を入れて言おう。

1. _____ _____ black.   わたしは黒色が好きです。

2. _____ _____ _____ green.   わたしは緑色が好きではありません。

3. _____ _____ _____ math?   あなたは算数が好きですか。

   – _____ , ____ _____.   — はい、好きです。

   – _____ , ____ _____.   — いいえ、好きではありません。

33

UNIT 6

Target Sentences

I play tennis.	わたしはテニスをします。
I don't play tennis.	私はテニスをしません。
Do you play baseball?	あなたは野球をしますか。
- Yes, I do.	- はい、します。
Do you play rugby?	あなたはラグビーをしますか。
- No, I don't.	- いいえ、しません。

1 よく聞いて、くりかえし言おう。

大問1

tennis	テニス
soccer	サッカー
rugby	ラグビー
baseball	野球
basketball	バスケットボール
dodgeball	ドッジボール
badminton	バドミントン
volleyball	バレーボール

大問2

2 聞こえてきた順番を数字で書こう。

1.  ( ) ( ) ( ) ( )

2. ( ) ( ) ( ) ( )

3. ( ) ( )  ( ) ( )

3 イラストのスポーツを表す英語を見つけて( )に番号を書こう。

( )

( )

( )

( )

( )

( )

( )

( )

1. baseball

2. tennis

3. soccer

4. volleyball

5. basketball

6. badminton

7. dodgeball

8. rugby

4 よく聞いて、くりかえし言おう。

大問4

> I play baseball.
> (わたしは野球をします。)

> I **don't** play baseball.
> (わたしは野球をしません。)

1. I play soccer.   I **don't** play soccer.

2. I play basketball.   I **don't** play basketball.

3. I play volleyball.   I **don't** play volleyball.

4. I play tennis.   I **don't** play tennis.

35

5 よく聞いて、くりかえし言おう。

Do you play soccer?

Yes, I do.

Do you play baseball?

No, I don't.

6 よく聞いて、次の質問に対する自分の答えを言おう。

1. Do you play soccer?   - Yes, I do. / No, I don't.

2. Do you play basketball?   - Yes, I do. / No, I don't.

3. Do you play baseball?   - Yes, I do. / No, I don't.

4. Do you play tennis?   - Yes, I do. / No, I don't.

5. Do you play rugby?   - Yes, I do. / No, I don't.

6. Do you play dodgeball?   - Yes, I do. / No, I don't.

7 よく聞いて、くりかえし言おう。

Do you play baseball?

  Baseball?

  Yes, I do. I like baseball very much.

Do you play tennis?

  Tennis?

  No, I don't. I don't like tennis.

Do you like rugby?

  Rugby?

  Yes, I do. I play rugby every day.

Do you like soccer?

  Soccer?

  No, I don't. I don't play soccer.

36

8 よく聞いて、Fred, Alice, Kenta になりきって英語を読もう。

大問8

Alice, do you play soccer?

Soccer? Yes, I do.
I like soccer very much.
I play soccer every day.

Kenta, do you play baseball?

No, I don't. I don't play baseball.
I like soccer very much.
I play soccer every day.

9 よく聞いて、それぞれがするスポーツを線でつなごう。

大問9

1. Emily ・

2. Fred ・

3. Jack ・

4. Alice ・

37

Key Points 英語、日本語の順に声に出して読もう。

I play …	I don't play …	Do you play…?
わたしは…をします。	わたしは…をしません。	あなたは…をしますか。
I play baseball. 　わたしは野球をします	I don't play rugby. 　わたしはラグビーをしません。	Do you play baseball? 　あなたは野球をしますか。 Yes, I do. 　- はい、します。 No, I don't. 　- いいえ、しません。

10 自分がするスポーツは I play…、しないスポーツは I don't play…で言おう。

tennis

basketball

rugby

soccer

dodgeball

baseball

badminton

volleyball

I play _____.　　I don't play_____.

_____.　　_____.

_____.　　_____.

_____.　　_____.

_____.　　_____.

11 英語をなぞろう。

I play soccer.

I don't play soccer.

Do you play soccer?

- Yes, I do.

- No, I don't.

12 日本語にあうように＿＿＿＿に英語を入れて言おう。

1. ＿＿＿ ＿＿＿＿＿＿ soccer.　　　　　わたしはサッカーをします。

2. ＿＿＿ ＿＿＿＿＿ ＿＿＿ soccer.　　　わたしはサッカーをしません。

3. ＿＿＿ ＿＿＿ ＿＿＿ soccer?　　　　あなたはサッカーをしますか。

- ＿＿＿ , ＿＿ ＿＿＿ .　　　　　　—はい、します。

- ＿＿＿ , ＿＿ ＿＿＿ .　　　　　　—いいえ、しません。

39

UNIT 7

Target Sentences

I have a cat.	わたしはネコをかっています。
I don't have a rabbit.	わたしはウサギをかっていません。
Do you have a dog?	あなたはイヌをかっていますか。
- Yes, I do.	- はい、かっています。
Do you have a goldfish?	あなたはキンギョをかっていますか
- No, I don't.	- いいえ、かっていません。

1 よく聞いて、くりかえし言おう。

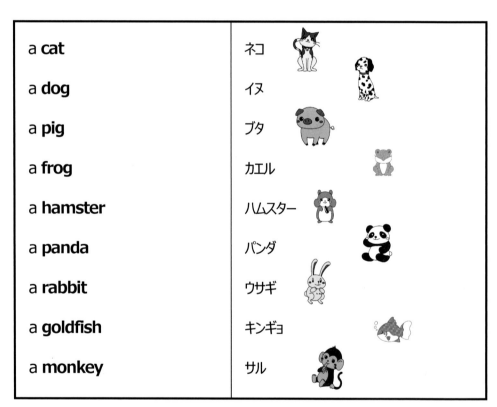

a **cat**	ネコ
a **dog**	イヌ
a **pig**	ブタ
a **frog**	カエル
a **hamster**	ハムスター
a **panda**	パンダ
a **rabbit**	ウサギ
a **goldfish**	キンギョ
a **monkey**	サル

2 聞こえてきた順番を数字で書こう。

大問2

1. a cat ( ) a dog ( ) a pig ( ) a goldfish ( )

2. a frog ( ) a panda ( ) a rabbit ( ) a monkey ( )

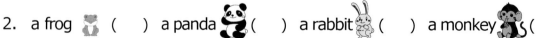

40

3 例にならって、イラストの動物と英語を結ぼう。

1. cat
2. pig
3. frog
4. dog

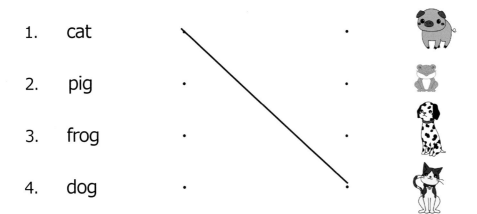

4 例にならって、イラストの動物になるよう線で結ぼう。

1. ham ・   ・ da ・   ・
2. pan ・   ・ fish ・   ・
3. rab ・   ・ key ・   ・
4. gold ・   ・ ster ・   ・
5. mon ・   ・ bit ・   ・

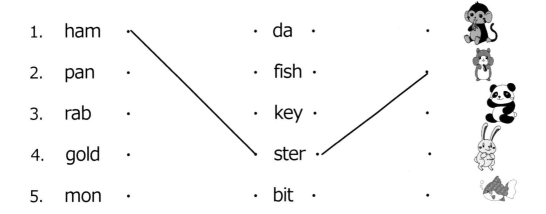

5 イラストの動物の名前をます目に入れてみよう。最後に水色のます目を上から読んで、その動物の
イラストを〇の中にかいてみよう。

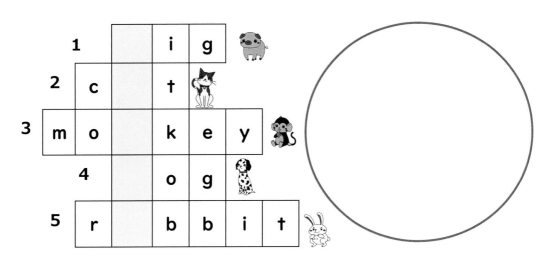

41

6 よく聞いて、くりかえし言おう。

| I have a cat.
（わたしはネコをかっています。） | I **don't** have a cat.
（わたしはネコをかっていません。） |

1. I have a dog.　　　　　　　　　I **don't** have a dog.

2. I have a rabbit.　　　　　　　I **don't** have a rabbit.

3. I have a hamster.　　　　　　I **don't** have a hamster.

4. I have a frog.　　　　　　　　I **don't** have a frog.

5. I have a goldfish.　　　　　　I **don't** have a goldfish.

7 よく聞いて、次の質問(しつもん)に対する自分の答えを言おう。

1. Do you have a cat? 　　Yes, I do.　/　No, I don't.

2. Do you have a dog? 　　Yes, I do.　/　No, I don't.

3. Do you have a rabbit? 　　Yes, I do.　/　No, I don't.

4. Do you have a hamster? 　　Yes, I do.　/　No, I don't.

5. Do you have a frog? 　　Yes, I do.　/　No, I don't.

6. Do you have a goldfish?　　Yes, I do.　/　No, I don't.

8 よく聞いて、その動物をかっていれば○、かっていなければ×をつけよう。

1.   2.   3.   4.   5.   6.

(　　)　　(　　)　　(　　)　　(　　)　　(　　)　　(　　)

9 例にならって、質問文を作ろう。次に自分にあてはめて Yes か No にしるし(✔)をつけ、質問文と答えを練習しよう。

Do you have a cat?

No, I don't.

	Yes	No
a cat		✔
a dog		
a hamster		
a rabbit		
a goldfish		

10 よく聞いて、くりかえし言おう。

Do you have a cat?

    Yes, I do.   I have a blue cat.

Blue cat!   Oh, no!

Do you have a dog?

    Yes, I do.   I have a pink dog.

Pink dog!   Oh, no!

Do you have a frog?

    Yes, I do.   I have a green frog.

Green frog!   Oh, yes!

I have a green frog too.

Key Points 英語、日本語の順に声に出して読もう。

I have …	I don't have …	Do you have … ?
わたしは…をもっています。 　　　　　（かっています）	わたしは…をもっていません。 　　　　　（かっていません）	あなたは…をもっていますか。 　　　　　（かっていますか）
I have a dog. わたしはイヌをかっています。	I don't have a dog. わたしはイヌをかっていません。	Do you have a dog? 　あなたはイヌをかっていますか。 Yes, I do. 　- はい、かっています。 No, I don't. 　- いいえ、かっていません。

44

11 イラストの動物を使って、自分がかっていれば I have… 、かっていなければ I don't have… を練習しよう。言えた動物には(　　)に✓を入れよう。

I have a cat.

I don't have a cat.

(　　) 　　(　　) 　　(　　) 　(　　) 　(　　)

(　　) 　　(　　) 　　(　　) 　(　　)

12 例にならって、正しい順番になるよう(　　)に番号を入れよう。

例)　a cat　-　I　-　have .
　　(3)　(1)　(2)

1.　have　-　you　　-　a frog　-　Do - ?
　　(　　)　(　　)　　(　　)　(　　)

2.　a hamster -　I　-　have　-　don't - .
　　(　　)　　(　　)　(　　)　(　　)

13 英語をなぞろう。

I have a dog.

I don't have a cat.

Do you have a frog?

- Yes, I do.

- No, I don't.

14 日本語にあうように、_____ に英語を入れて言おう。

1. _____ _____ a dog.　　わたしはイヌをかっています。

2. ____ _____ _____ a cat.　　わたしはネコをかっていません。

3. ____ _____ _____ a frog?　　あなたはカエルをかっていますか。

　- _____ , ___ _____ .　　— はい、かっています。

　- _____ , ___ _____ .　　— いいえ、かっていません。

EXTRA (UNIT 5 – UNIT 7)

1 Fred が Alice に質問をしています。国、動物、教科、色、数字に関する単語を消していき、
残った単語を並べかえて、Fred の質問と Alice の答えを作ろう。

twelve	a panda	one	music
the UK	Do	Japanese	yellow
China	eight	like	green
four	P.E.	a hamster	seven
you	eleven	baseball	Australia

＿＿＿＿＿ ＿＿＿＿＿ ＿＿＿＿＿ ＿＿＿＿＿ ?

math	a monkey	black	music
Japan	I	three	a cat
the USA	two	Yes	pink
nine	science	a goldfish	ten
do	orange	blue	Canada

＿＿＿＿＿ , ＿＿＿＿＿ ＿＿＿＿＿ .

3 次の国では虹は何色に見えているのだろう。（　　）の色をぬろう。

Taiwan（red, yellow, purple）
（ブヌン族）

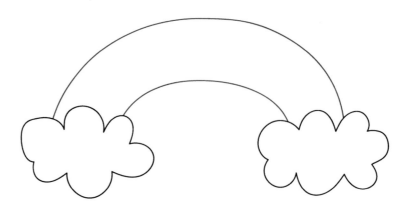

Indonesia（red, yellow, green, blue）
（フローレス島）

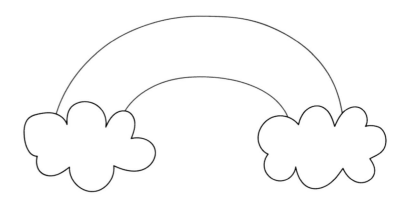

Japan（何色か考えよう！）

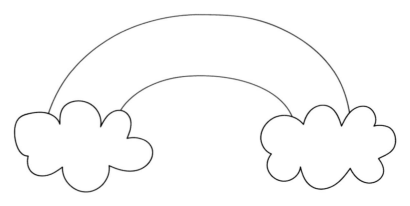

48

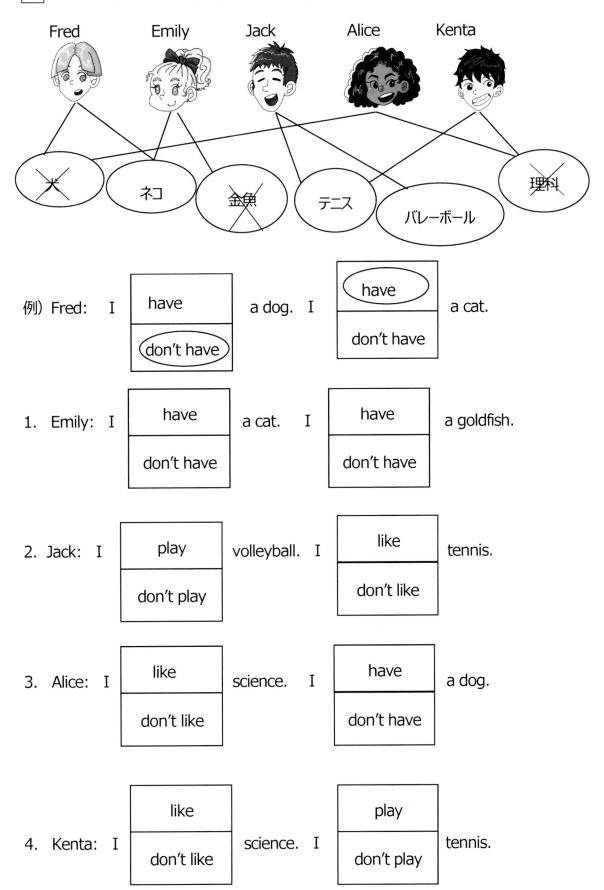

4 例にならって、それぞれの人物になりきって、英語で言おう。

| Fred | Emily | Jack | Alice | Kenta |

米 　ネコ　 金魚　 テニス　 バレーボール　 理科

例) Fred: I 　[have / (don't have)] 　a dog. I 　[(have) / don't have] 　a cat.

1. Emily: I 　[have / don't have] 　a cat. I 　[have / don't have] 　a goldfish.

2. Jack: I 　[play / don't play] 　volleyball. I 　[like / don't like] 　tennis.

3. Alice: I 　[like / don't like] 　science. I 　[have / don't have] 　a dog.

4. Kenta: I 　[like / don't like] 　science. I 　[play / don't play] 　tennis.

49

5 例にならって、正しい順番になるよう( )に番号を入れよう。

例）your – name – What's - ?
　　（ 2 ）　（ 3 ）　（ 1 ）

1. like　–　I　–　　social studies　– .
　　（　）　（　）　　（　）

2. I　–　a　–　have　–　rabbit　– .
　　（　）　（　）　（　）　　（　）

3. play –　Do　–　you – dodgeball - ?
　　（　）　（　）　（　）　　（　）

4. like　–　yellow　–　I　–　don't　– .
　　（　）　　（　）　　（　）　（　）

5. Where　–　from　–　you　–　are　– ?
　　（　）　　（　）　（　）　（　）

大問6

6 よく聞いて、英語の内容（ないよう）と合うイラストを見つけて( )にアルファベットを書こう。

　　　A　　　　　　　　B　　　　　　　　C　　　　　　　　D

1. (　　)　　　2. (　　)　　　3. (　　)　　　4. (　　)

7 例にならって、自分のことについてできるだけたくさん英語で言おう。

例) I like soccer.　I don't play volleyball.　I am ten.

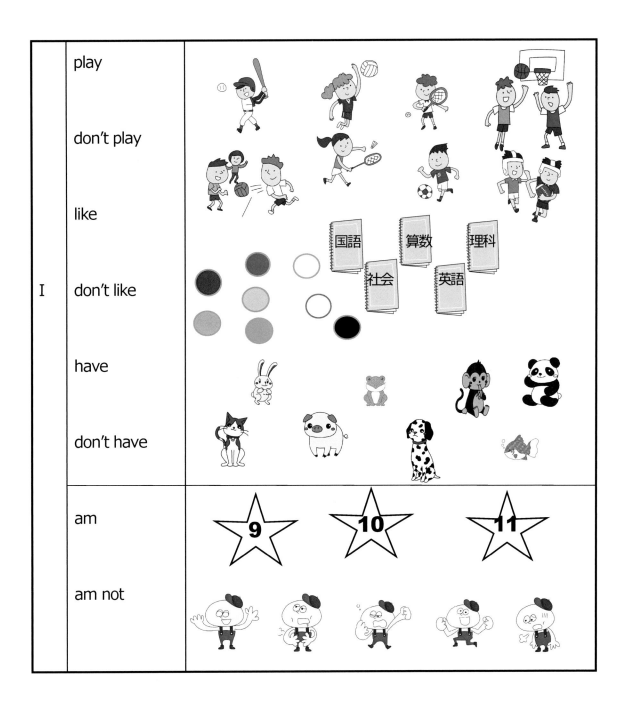

8 交流校のお友達からメッセージが届きました。メッセージを聞こう。

> Hi!
> My name is Lucy. I'm twelve. Who are you?
> How old are you?
>
> I'm from the UK. Where are you from?
>
> I play soccer every Sunday. I like soccer.
> Do you like soccer?
>
> Please write soon!
>
> Lucy

every Sunday 毎週日曜日

Please write soon. 返事をちょうだいね。

Lucy に返事を書いてみよう。

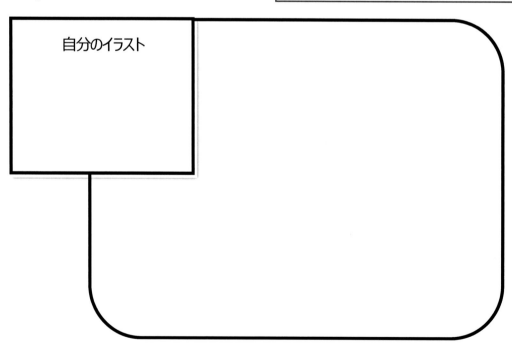

自分のイラスト

UNIT 8

Target Sentences

Can you run fast?	あなたは速く走ることができますか。
- Yes, I can.　I can run fast.	- はい、できます。速く走ることができます。
Can you jump high?	あなたは高くジャンプすることができますか。
- No, I can't.	- いいえ、できません。
I can't jump high.	高くジャンプすることはできません。
Can you sing well?	あなたはじょうずに歌うことができますか。
- Yes, I can.　I can sing well.	- はい、できます。じょうずに歌うことができます。

大問1

1 よく聞いて、くりかえし言おう。

play	演奏する
play the **recorder**	**リコーダー**を吹く
ride	乗る
ride a **bicycle (bike)**	**自転車**に乗る
jump	ジャンプする
jump **high**	**高く**ジャンプする
run	走る
run **fast**	**速く**走る
sing	歌う
sing **well**	**じょうずに**歌う
swim	泳ぐ
skate	スケートする
ski	スキーする
cook	料理する
dance	おどる

53

2 例にならって、英語とイラストを結ぼう。

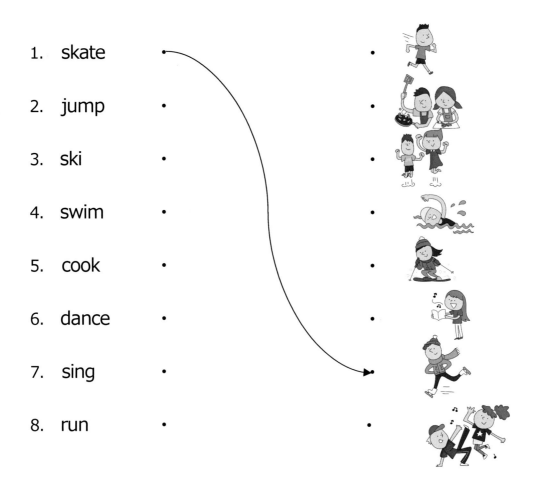

1. skate
2. jump
3. ski
4. swim
5. cook
6. dance
7. sing
8. run

3 右からあてはまる英語を選んで、左の表を完成させよう。

r		
	k	
c		k
	u	m
s	w	

jump
swim
ski
cook
run

54

4 聞こえてきた順番を数字で書こう。

1.  (　)  (　)  (　)  (　)

2. (　)  (　)  (　)  (　)

5 例にならって、英語と日本語を線で結ぼう。

1. play the recorder　・   ・ 自転車に乗る

2. ride a bicycle　・   ・ じょうずに歌う

3. jump high　・   ・ 速く走る

4. run fast　・   ・ リコーダーを吹く

5. sing well　・   ・ 高くジャンプする

6 よく聞いて、質問に対する自分の答えを〇で囲もう。

1. Can you dance well?　　　　Yes, I can.　/　No, I can't.

2. Can you swim fast?　　　　Yes, I can.　/　No, I can't.

3. Can you jump high?　　　　Yes, I can.　/　No, I can't.

4. Can you ride a bicycle?　　Yes, I can.　/　No, I can't.

5. Can you play the recorder?　Yes, I can.　/　No, I can't.

7 イラストにあうように ＿＿＿＿ に I can か I can't を入れて言おう。

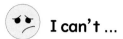 😄 I can ...   😞 I can't ...

1. ＿＿＿＿＿＿＿＿＿＿ skate.

2. ＿＿＿＿＿＿＿＿＿＿ cook well.

3. ＿＿＿＿＿＿＿＿＿＿ swim.

4. ＿＿＿＿＿＿＿＿＿＿ run fast.

5. ＿＿＿＿＿＿＿＿＿＿ play the recorder.

6. ＿＿＿＿＿＿＿＿＿＿ ride a bike.

大問8

8 よく聞いて、くりかえして言おう。

Can you cook?

    Yes, I can.

    I can cook *miso* soup.

Can you dance?

    Yes, I can.

    I can dance hip hop.
<small>ヒップ　ホップ</small>

Can you skate?

    Yes, I can.

    Let's skate together.
<small>〜しましょう　　いっしょに</small>

Can you swim?

    Yes, I can.

    Let's swim together.

9 よく聞いて、質問文と答えをくりかえして言おう。次に Kenta, Ana, Emily になりきって
質問に答えよう。

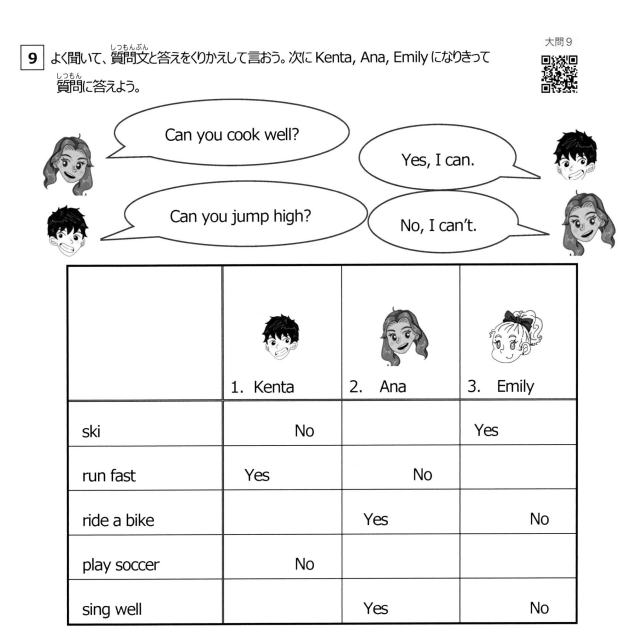

Can you cook well?

Yes, I can.

Can you jump high?

No, I can't.

	1. Kenta	2. Ana	3. Emily
ski	No		Yes
run fast	Yes	No	
ride a bike		Yes	No
play soccer	No		
sing well		Yes	No

Key Points 英語、日本語の順に声に出して読もう。

I can …	I can't …	Can you … ?
わたしは…できます。	わたしは…できません。	あなたは…できますか。
I can run fast. わたしは速く走ることができます。	I can't run fast. わたしは速く走ることができません。	Can you run fast? あなたは速く走ることができますか。 　　-Yes, I can. 　　　はい、できます。 　　-No, I can't. 　　　いいえ、できません。

10 イラストを使って、いろいろな文を作って言おう。

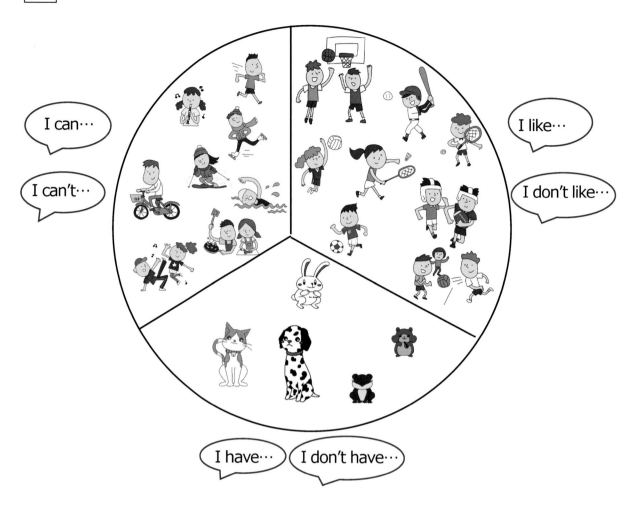

I can…

I can't…

I like…

I don't like…

I have… I don't have…

11 例にならって、正しい順番になるよう（　）に番号を入れよう。

例）your – name – What's – ?

（ 2 ）（ 3 ）　（ 1 ）

1. fast – can – I – run –.

（　）（　）（　）（　）

2. sing – Can – well – you – ?

（　）（　）（　）（　）

3. can't – I – high – jump –.

（　）（　）（　）（　）

12 英語をなぞろう。

I can play the recorder.

I can't run fast.

Can you jump high?

- Yes, I can.

- No, I can't.

13 日本語にあうように_____に英語を入れて言おう。

1. I _____ _____the recorder. わたしはリコーダーを吹くことができます。

2. I _____ _____ fast. わたしは速く走ることができません。

3. _____ _____ _____ high? あなたは高くジャンプすることができますか。

4. -_____ , ____ _____. ―はい、できます。

5. -_____ , ____ _____. ―いいえ、できません。

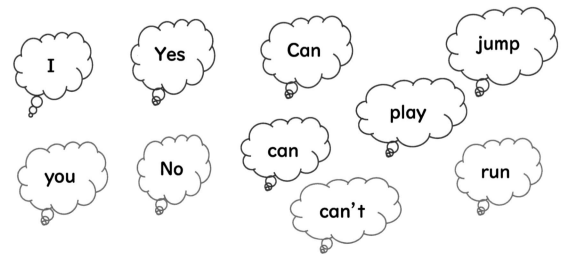

59

UNIT 9

Target Sentences

The pen is on the desk.	ペンは机（つくえ）の上にあります。
The book is in the bag.	本はかばんの中にあります。
The ruler is under the desk.	ものさしは机（つくえ）の下にあります。

1 よく聞いて、くりかえし言おう。

a **pen**	ペン
a **pencil**	えんぴつ
a **ruler**	ものさし
a **pencil case**	ふでばこ
a **book**	本
a **notebook**	ノート
a **bag**	かばん
a **desk**	机（つくえ）
a **chair**	いす
on	…の上に
in	…の中に
under	…の下に

2 聞こえてきた順番を数字で書こう。

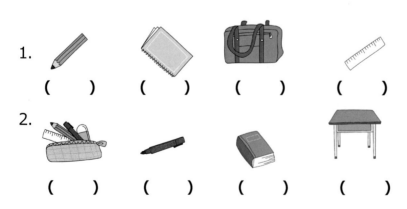

1. (　　)　(　　)　(　　)　(　　)

2. (　　)　(　　)　(　　)　(　　)

3 例にならって、英語とイラストを結ぼう。

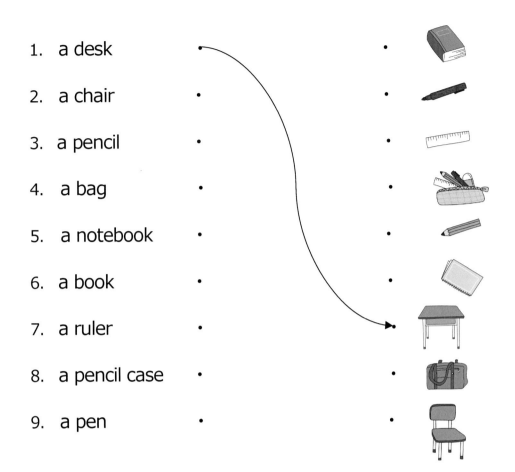

1. a desk

2. a chair

3. a pencil

4. a bag

5. a notebook

6. a book

7. a ruler

8. a pencil case

9. a pen

大問4

4 よく聞いて、くりかえし言おう。

The cat is **in** the bag.

The cat is **on** the desk.

The cat is **under** the chair.

61

6 イラストにあうように＿＿に in、 on、 under のうちのどれかを〇で囲み、言おう。

例)

The pencil is { (in) / on / under } the bag.

1. The book is { in / on / under } the chair.

2. The notebook is { in / on / under } the book.

3. The ruler is { in / on / under } the pencil case.

4. The pen is { in / on / under } the desk.

5. The pen is { in / on / under } the chair.

6. The ruler is { in / on / under } the book.

7 音声に続いて、ジェスチャーをしながらくりかえし言おう。

In, on, under.   in   on   under

In, on, under.

In, on, under.

ジェスチャーをしながらくりかえし言おう。

1. on ➡ in ➡ under

2. under ➡ on ➡ in

3. in ➡ under ➡ on

4. on ➡ under ➡ in

8 よく聞いて、2つのうち正しいイラストを選んで( )に〇をつけよう。

1.

( )   ( )

2.

( )   ( )

3.

( )   ( )

4.

( )   ( )

9 イラストにあうように、〇か×を ☐ に書こう。

1. The cat is on the notebook. ☐

2. The pencil is on the desk. ☐

3. The apple is in the plastic bag. (ビニール ふくろ) ☐

4. The pencil case is in the desk. ☐

5. The book is under the chair. ☐

6. The pen is on the chair. ☐

Key Points 英語、日本語の順に声に出して読もう。

in (〜の中に)	on(〜の上に)	under(〜の下に)
The cat is in the bag.	The cat is on the desk.	The cat is under the chair.
ネコはかばんの中にいます。	ネコは机の上にいます。	ネコはいすの下にいます。

| The ☐ is { in / on / under } 〜 | ☐ は〜の { 中 / 上 / 下 } にあります・います。 |

10 in, on, under と ▢ の中の英語を組み合わせて、自由に文を作って言おう。イラストもかこう。

cat	dog	frog	hamster	monkey
pencil	book	ruler	notebook	
bag	chair	desk	pencil case	

(   ) (   )   *(   )には自由に書こう。

例) **The <u>frog</u> is <u>on</u> the <u>book</u>.** カエルは本の上にいます。

1. The _____ is _____the_____.

2. The _____ is _____the_____.

3. The _____ is _____the_____.

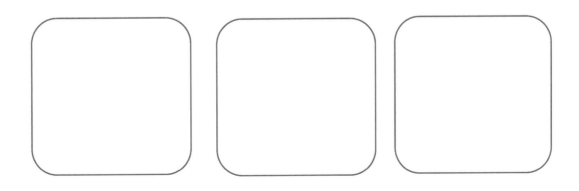

            1   2   3

11 英語をなぞろう。

The bag is on the desk.

The book is in the bag.

The pencil is under the desk.

UNIT 10

Target Sentences

How many apples do you have?　　あなたはリンゴを何こ持っていますか。

　- I have ten apples.　　　　　　 － 10こ持っています。

---

1 よく聞いて、くりかえし言おう。

大問1

a **banana**	バナナ	
a **melon**	メロン	
a **strawberry**	イチゴ	
a **carrot**	ニンジン	
a **radish**	ダイコン	
a **potato**	ジャガイモ	
a **tomato**	トマト	
an **apple**	リンゴ	
an **orange**	オレンジ	
an **onion**	タマネギ	
How many…?	いくつ…ですか。	

---

a は「1つ、1人」の意味を表す。

　　　a banana　a melon　a potato

あとに続く単語が母音(**a i u e o**)で始まるときは、**an** を使う。

　　　an apple　an orange　an onion

67

2 a か an に○をつけよう。

1. a / an **b**anana
2. a / an **r**adish
3. a / an **a**pple
4. a / an **m**elon
5. a / an **o**nion
6. a / an **t**omato
7. a / an **p**otato
8. a / an **o**range
9. a /an **c**arrot
10. a / an **s**trawberry

3 よく聞いて、くりかえし言おう。

an apple　apple**s**　　**a** banana　banana**s**

a melon　melon**s**　　**a** strawberry　strawberr**ies**

an orange　orange**s**　　**a** carrot　carrot**s**

an onion　onion**s**　　**a** radish　radish**es**

a potato　potato**es**　　**a** tomato　tomato**es**

4 聞こえてきた順番を数字で書こう。

1. a banana 🍌   an orange 🍊   an apple 🍎   a strawberry 🍓
   (   )   (   )   (   )   (   )

2. an onion 🧅   a carrot 🥕   a radish   a tomato 🍅
   (   )   (   )   (   )   (   )

3. strawberries   bananas   oranges   melons
   (   )   (   )   (   )   (   )

4. carrots   potatoes   onions   radishes
   (   )   (   )   (   )   (   )

5 複数(1つより多い数)の形をした英語をたどろう。

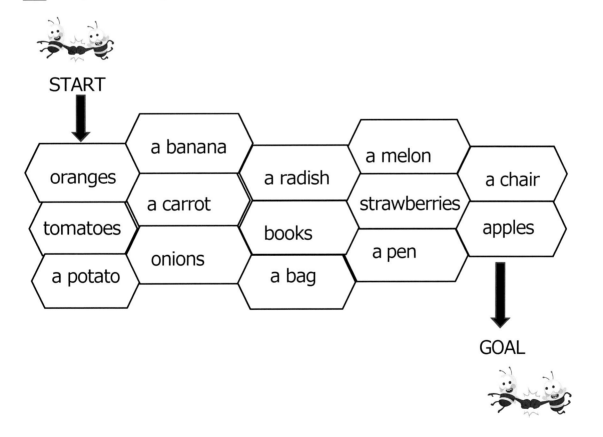

START

oranges	a banana	a radish	a melon	a chair
tomatoes	a carrot	books	strawberries	apples
a potato	onions	a bag	a pen	

GOAL

6 クロスワード。色のついたます目を上から読んでみよう。そのくだものが I like _____.の答えです。

1   2   3

		t	o		a	t	o	e	s
2	s	t	r	a	w	b		r	r	i	e	s

1 | t | o | | a | t | o | e | s
2 s | t | r | a | w | b | | r | r | i | e | s
3 | a | p | p | | e | s
4 | o | n | i | | n | s
5 | b | a | n | a | | a | s
6 p | o | t | a | t | o | e

4   5   6

7   **I like** _____.

7 よく聞いて、くりかえし言おう。

How many apples do you have?

I have <u>four</u> apples.

下の英語を使って、「いくつ持っていますか」の質問と答えを練習しよう。

1. <u>bananas</u> / <u>three</u>

2. <u>strawberries</u> / <u>ten</u>

3. <u>potatoes</u> / <u>five</u>

4. <u>melons</u> / <u>two</u>

5. <u>onions</u> / <u>seven</u>

6. <u>radishes</u> / <u>eight</u>

8 よく聞いて、質問文と答えをくりかえし言おう。次に、Kenta, Fred, Alice になりきって、質問に答えよう。

例) How many <u>pencils</u> do you have?

  - I have <u>seven</u> pencils.

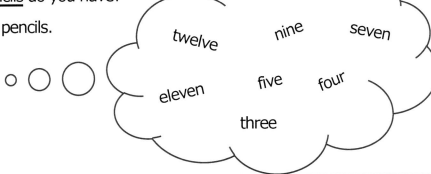

twelve   nine   seven
eleven   five   four
three

	1. Kenta	2. Fred	3. Alice
pencils	seven	twelve	nine
notebooks	five	eight	seven
books	two	eleven	three
pens	three	six	eleven

9 よく聞いて、くりかえし言おう。

How many potatoes do you have?

  -I have three.

That's OK. (それでだいじょうぶ)

How many onions do you have?

  -I have one.

That's OK.

How many sausages (ソーセージ) do you have?

  -I have eight.

That's perfect! (かんぺき)

Now let's make stew! (さあ、シチューを作りましょう)

71

Key Points　英語、日本語の順に声に出して読んでみよう。

an orange	orange**s**
a book	book**s**
a radish	radish**es**

How many apples do you have?

あなたはリンゴを何に持っていますか。

-I have an apple.

1ご持っています。

-I have six apples.

6ご持っています。

---

10 英語をなぞろう。

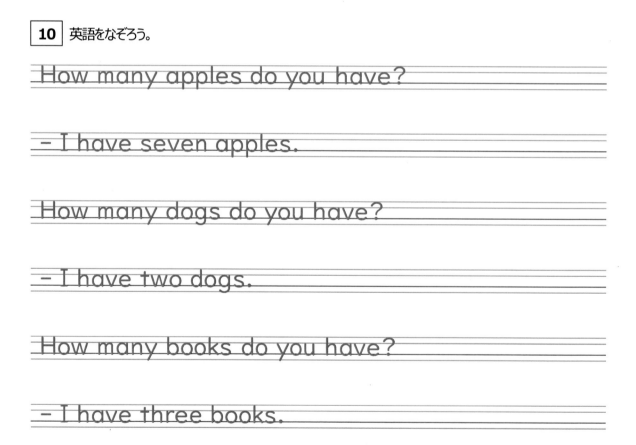

How many apples do you have?

- I have seven apples.

How many dogs do you have?

- I have two dogs.

How many books do you have?

- I have three books.

72

11 日本語にあうように_____に英語を入れて言おう。

1. _____ many apples do you have?　　あなたはリンゴを何こ持っていますか。

　　- I have seven _____.　　- 7こ持っています。

2. How_____ dogs do you have?　　あなたは犬を何匹かっていますか。

　　- I have _____ dogs.　　- 2匹かっています。

3. _____ _____ books do you have?　　あなたは本を何さつ持っていますか。

　　- I have _____ books.　　- 3さつ持っています。

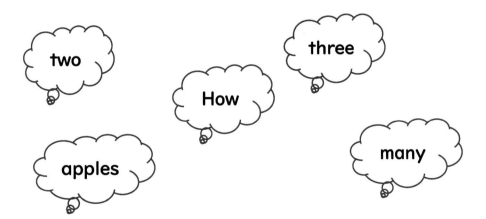

two

three

How

apples

many

73

EXTRA (UNIT 8 – UNIT 10)

1 Ana と Fred が持ち物の場所をたずねあいしています。例にならって、どこにあるか_____に On, In, Under のいずれかを入れよう。

例)

Where is my ruler?
_{どこにありますか}

__In__ the pencil case.

1. Where is my book?

   _____the desk.

2. Where is my cat?

   _____ the chair.

3. Where is my notebook?

   _____the bag.

4. Where is my pencil?

   _____the desk.

5. Where is my dog?

   _____the chair.

2 イラストにあう文を選び、＿＿＿にアルファベットを書こう。

1. ＿＿＿＿＿

2. ＿＿＿＿＿

3. ＿＿＿＿＿

4. ＿＿＿＿＿

5. ＿＿＿＿＿

A.　The rabbit is under the desk.

B.　The book is on the chair.

C.　The pig is in the desk.

D.　The hamster is on the book.

E.　The melon is on the tomato.

F.　The dog is in the bag.

G.　The apple is on the melon.

H.　The frog is on the chair.

3 イラストを参考に右から英語を選んで、＿＿＿＿に書こう。

1. **Can you** ＿＿＿＿＿＿＿＿＿＿ **well?**

2. **Can you** ＿＿＿＿＿＿＿＿＿＿ **the recorder?**

3. **Can you** ＿＿＿＿＿＿＿＿＿＿ **a bicycle?**

4. **Can you** ＿＿＿＿＿＿＿＿＿＿ **fast?**

5. **Can you** ＿＿＿＿＿＿＿＿＿＿ **high?**

6. **Can you** ＿＿＿＿＿＿＿＿＿＿ *miso* **soup?**

jump

cook

ride

run

sing

play

4 自分ができることと、できないことを □ から選んで、英語で書いて言おう。

  *[   ]には自由に書こう

I can…

_____

_____

_____

I can't…

_____

_____

_____

play soccer
　　volleyball
　　tennis
　　[   ]

play the recorder
　　　ピアノ
　　the piano
　　　カスタネット
　　the castanet
　　[   ]

cook *takoyaki*
　　ramen
　　miso soup
　　[   ]

5 Can you…?の質問に対する自分の答えを **Yes, I can.** か **No, I can't.** で言おう。

1. **Can you cook *sukiyaki*?**　　　_____, ___ _____.

2. **Can you play volleyball?**　　　_____, ___ _____.

3. **Can you sing English songs?**　_____, ___ _____.

4. **Can you ski well?**　　　　　_____, ___ _____.

6 例にならって、複数形で言おう。

(例) **a banana** ➡ **bananas**

a melon ➡ _____

a carrot ➡ _____

a book ➡ _____

a chair ➡ _____

a pencil ➡ _____

(例) **an apple** ➡ **apples**

an orange ➡ _____

an onion ➡ _____

7 Alice と Fred が話をしています。日本語にあうように_____に英語を入れよう。

Hi, Fred. How are you?　　　　　　　やあ、フレッド。元気？

I'm fine, thank you.　And you?　　　元気だよ、ありがとう。きみは？

OK, thank you.　　　　　　　　　　元気よ、ありがとう。

_____ you have a dog?　　　イヌをかってるの？

No, I _____.　　　　　　　いいや、かってないよ。

_____ _____ have a cat?　　ネコはかってるの？

Yes, I _____.　　　　　　　うん、かってるよ。

_____ _____ cats do you have?　何匹ネコをかってるの？

I have _____ cats.　　　　　5匹かってるよ。

I have _____ white cats and　白ネコ2匹と

_____ black cats.　　　　　黒ネコ3匹かってるんだ。

Do you have a cat?　　　　　　　　きみはネコをかってる？

_____, I do.　　　　　　　ええ、かっているわ。

I have _____ cats!　　　　　10匹かってるの！

Wow!　　　　　　　　　　　　　わ～！

8 次の単語を3つずつグループにわけよう。

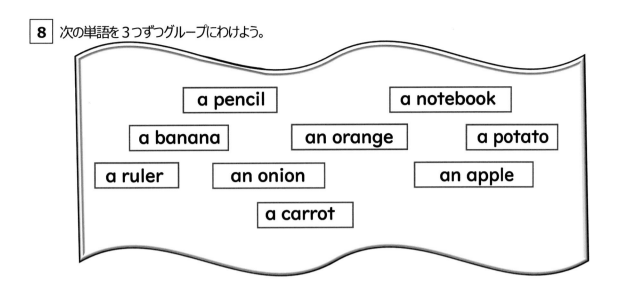

a pencil　　a notebook
a banana　　an orange　　a potato
a ruler　　an onion　　an apple
a carrot

Fruits(果物)	Vegetables(野菜)	Stationery(文ぼう具)

9 知っている単語を○で囲もう。

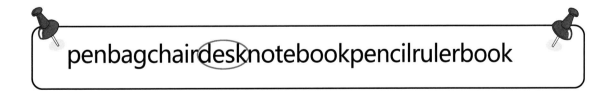

penbagchairdesknotebookpencilrulerbook

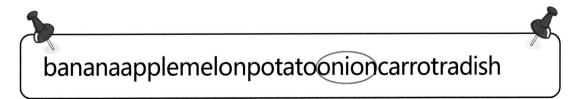

bananaapplemelonpotatoonioncarrotradish

10 よく聞いて、Mary, Tom, Jeff, Alice がそれぞれ何をいくつ持っているか、線で結ぼう。

1. Mary ・   ・ 2 ・   ・ bags

2. Tom ・   ・ 4 ・   ・ books

3. Jeff ・   ・ 7 ・   ・ pencils

4. Alice ・   ・ 9 ・   ・ notebooks

                   ・ 10 ・   ・ rulers

11 それぞれの質問の答えを選んで、＿＿＿にその番号を書こう。

1. Where's my notebook? ＿＿＿＿＿

2. How many pencils do you have? ＿＿＿＿＿

3. Do you have a dog? ＿＿＿＿＿

4. Can you dance well? ＿＿＿＿＿

5. Are you hungry? ＿＿＿＿＿

①No, I can't.

②No, I don't.

③It's on the desk.

④Yes, I am.

⑤I have five.

UNIT 11

Target Sentences

Target Sentences

> Ed is my brother. He is tall.
>
> Lin is my friend. She is from China.
>
> エドはぼくのお兄さんです。彼は背が高いです。
>
> リンはわたしの友達です。彼女は中国出身です。

1 よく聞いて、くりかえし言おう。

大問1

family	家族
father	父
mother	母
brother	兄・弟
sister	姉・妹
grandpa	おじいさん、祖父
grandma	おばあさん、祖母
kind	やさしい
big	大きい
small	小さい
tall	背が高い
old	年をとっている
he	彼
she	彼女

大問2

2 聞こえてきた順に番号をつけよう。

brother (　　) father (　　) grandma(　　)

mother (　　) grandpa (　　) sister (　　)

3 例にならって、左の英語と右の日本語を線で結ぼう。

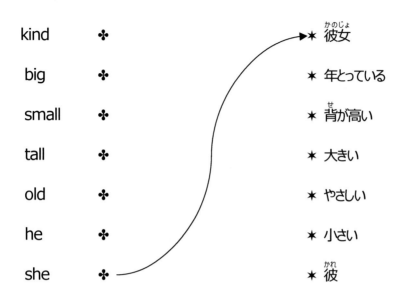

kind	❖		❖	彼女^{かのじょ}
big	❖		★	年とっている
small	❖		★	背^せが高い
tall	❖		★	大きい
old	❖		★	やさしい
he	❖		★	小さい
she	❖		★	彼^{かれ}

4 右からあてはまるアルファベットを選んで、左の表を完成させよう。

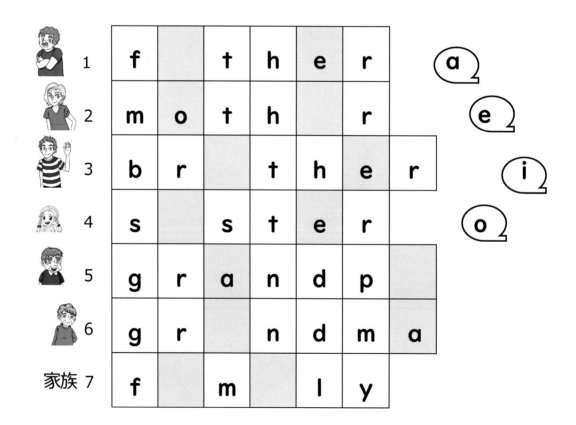

5 イラストの人物と he か she を線で結ぼう。

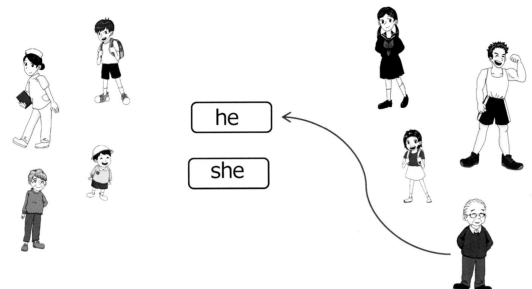

6 He か She に〇をつけよう。

1   2   3   4   5   6

1. This is my father.   [He / She] is big.

2. This is my mother.   [He / She] is kind.

3. This is my sister.   [He / She] is small.

4. This is my brother.   [He / She] is tall.

5. This is my grandpa.   [He / She] is old.

6. This is my grandma.   [He / She] is old.

7 _____ に He か She を書こう。

1. Mary is my sister. _____ is happy.

2. Jim is my brother. _____ is tired.

3. This is my grandpa. _____ is hungry.

4. This is my grandma. _____ is sleepy.

5. This is my father. _____ is fine.

8 よく聞いて、くりかえし言おう。

大問8

Hello.　I'm Jack.
This is my sister.
She is Meg.
She is kind.

Hello.　I'm Meg.
This is my brother.
He is Mike.
He is tall.

Hello.　I'm Mike.
This is my friend.
He is Bob.
He is happy.

9 例にならって、カードの人物を相手にしょうかいしよう。

例)

Kenta / my classmate / ten

1. Hana / my sister / nine

2. Fred / my friend / tall

3. Meg / my classmate / twelve

4. Ms. Brown / my teacher / from England

Key Points 英語、日本語の順に声に出して読んでみよう。

he 彼	she 彼女
This is **my father**. こちらはわたしの父です。 **He** is big. 彼は大きいです。	This is **my sister**. こちらはわたしの妹です。 **She** is Mary. 彼女はメアリーです。

10 英語を聞いて、am / are / is から正しいものを選んで〇で囲もう。

1. Bob [am / are / is] my brother.

2. Mary [am / are / is] my sister.

3. I [am / are / is] Chris.

4. You [am / are / is] my friend.

5. My father [am / are / is] big.

6. Ms. Sasaki [am / are / is] kind.

11 例にならって、いろいろな文を作って言おう。

例) **Ms. Brown is tall.   /   Alice is my friend.**

Kenta		my friend.
Alice		my teacher.
Mary		my classmate.
Fred	is	big.
Mr. (自分の先生の名前)		tall.
Ms. (自分の先生の名前)		kind.
(友達の名前)		from Australia.
(家族の名前)		twelve.
		( )
		( )

*(   )には自由に書こう。

作った英文を一つ選び、書こう。

86

12 英語をなぞろう。

This is my classmate.

He is Ken.

She is my friend.

My mother is tall.

My brother is kind.

13 日本語にあうように、＿＿＿に英語を入れて言おう。

1. ＿＿＿＿＿＿ ＿＿＿＿＿ my classmate.　　こちらはわたしのクラスメートです。

2. ＿＿＿＿＿＿ ＿＿＿＿＿ Chris.　　彼女^{かのじょ}はクリスです。

3. ＿＿＿＿＿＿ ＿＿＿＿ my friend.　　彼^{かれ}はわたしの友人です。

4. My mother ＿＿＿＿＿＿ ＿＿＿＿＿.　　わたしの母はやさしい。

5. My brother ＿＿＿＿＿＿ ＿＿＿＿＿.　　わたしの兄は背^せが高い。

87

UNIT 12

Target Sentences

> Where is Mary? メアリーはどこにいますか。
>
> - She's in the garden. - 彼女(かのじょ)は庭にいます。
>
> Where is Tom? トムはどこにいますか。
>
> - He's in the kitchen. - 彼(かれ)は台所にいます。
>
> Where is my cat? 私のネコはどこにいますか。
>
> - It's under the sofa. - ソファーの下にいます。

大問1

1 よく聞いて、くりかえし言おう。

a **bed**	ベッド
a **sofa**	ソファ
a **table**	テーブル
a **curtain**	カーテン
a **kitchen**	台所
a **bathroom**	浴室
a **living room**	居間(いま)・リビング
a **garden**	庭
by	〜のそばに
behind	〜のうしろに
he's (=he is)	彼(かれ)は〜です
she's (=she is)	彼女(かのじょ)は〜です

2 聞こえてきた順に番号をつけよう。

1.

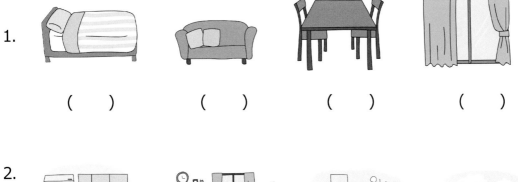

( )　　　　( )　　　　( )　　　　( )

2.

( )　　　　( )　　　　( )　　　　( )

3 例にならって、イラストにあう英語を見つけて結びつけよう。

1.

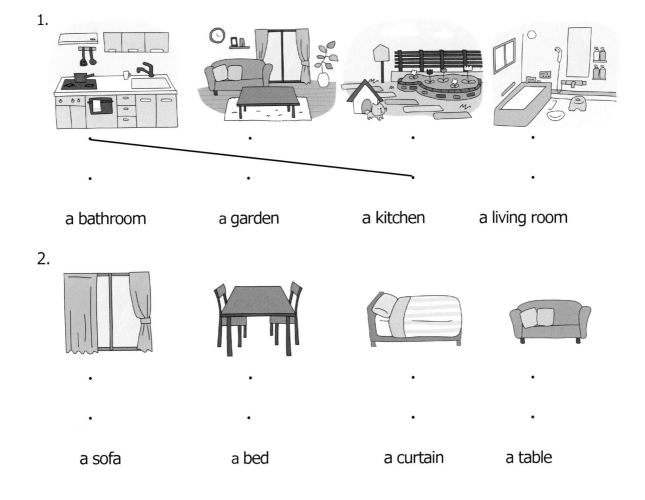

a bathroom　　　a garden　　　a kitchen　　　a living room

2.

a sofa　　　a bed　　　a curtain　　　a table

4 日本語のヒントを参考に、アルファベットを並べかえよう。

1. **d b e** → <u>b</u> <u>　　</u> <u>　　</u>　　ベッド

2. **f s a o** → <u>s</u> <u>　　</u> <u>f</u> <u>　　</u>　　ソファ

3. **a b e l t** → <u>t</u> <u>　　</u> <u>b</u> <u>l</u> <u>　　</u>　　テーブル

4. **i u a c t n r** → <u>c</u> <u>u</u> <u>r</u> <u>t</u> <u>　　</u> <u>　　</u> n　　カーテン

大問5

5 英語を聞いて、英語にあうイラストを選び、数字を書こう。

1. Pam is **in** the kitchen. <u>　　　　</u>

2. Pam is **on** the bed. <u>　　　　</u>

3. Pam is **under** the table. <u>　　　　</u>

4. Pam is **behind** the curtain. <u>　　　　</u>

5. Pam is **by** the chair. <u>　　　　</u>

①

②

③

④

⑤

6 イラストを表す英語を下から選んで言おう。

1. Pam is <u>　　　　</u> the chair.

2. Pam is <u>　　　　</u> the living room.

3. Pam is <u>　　　　</u> the bed.

4. Pam is <u>　　　　</u> the ^木tree.

by　　behind　　in　　under

90

7 よく聞いて、くりかえし言おう。

大問7

Where is Pam?

He's in the kitchen.

8 例にならって、イラストにあう正しい方を〇で囲もう。

Where is your father?

He's (in / on) the living room .

1. Where is your dog? — It's (on / under) the sofa.

2. Where is my cat? — It's (on / under) the table.

3. Where is Pam? — He's (behind / in) the curtain.

4. Where is your mother? — She's (by / behind) my father.

91

9 よく聞いて、くりかえし言おう。

Where is Mom?
_{お母さん}

In the kitchen?   - No.

In the living room?   - No.

Where is she?   - She's in the garden.

Oh, I see.
_{わかった}

Where is Dad?
_{お父さん}

In the garden?   - No.

In the bathroom?   - No.

Where is he?   - He's under the bed!

Oh, again!?
_{また}

Key Points   英語、日本語の順に声に出して読んでみよう。

Where is …?	He's(She's / It's) on/ in/ under/ behind….
…はどこにいますか。	上　中　下　　後ろ 彼(彼女 / それ)は…にいます。

10 英語をなぞろう。

Where is Ana?

She's in the kitchen.

Where is Kenta?

He's on the bed.

11 例にならって、Pam がどこにいるか順番に英語で言おう。

例

Pam is in the kitchen.

GOAL

the plastic bag

the tree

START

UNIT 13

Target Sentences

What day is it today?	今日は何曜日ですか。
- It's Sunday.	- 日曜日です。
What time is it now?	今、何時ですか。
- It's seven.	- 7時です。

1 よく聞いて、くりかえし言おう。

day	曜日、日、1日
today	今日
Sunday	日曜日
Monday	月曜日
Tuesday	火曜日
Wednesday	水曜日
Thursday	木曜日
Friday	金曜日
Saturday	土曜日
Sunday	日曜日
time	時間・時刻
now	今
It's (=It is) seven.	7時です。

2 英語をなぞってみよう。

1. 月曜日　Monday　　　　Monday

2. 火曜日　Tuesday　　　　Tuesday

3. 水曜日　Wednesday　　　Wednesday

4. 木曜日　Thursday　　　Thursday

5. 金曜日　Friday　　　　Friday

6. 土曜日　Saturday　　　Saturday

7. 日曜日　Sunday　　　　Sunday

大問3

3 よく聞いて、読まれた方の曜日に〇をつけよう。

1. Monday / Sunday 　　　2. Tuesday  / Thursday

3. Wednesday  / Saturday 　　4. Friday / Sunday

5. Saturday / Thursday

大問4

4 聞こえてきた順に番号をつけよう。

1. (　　)　　　(　　)　　　(　　)　　　(　　)

　Monday　　Tuesday　　Wednesday　　Thursday

2. (　　)　　　(　　)　　　(　　)　　　(　　)

　Thursday　　Friday　　Saturday　　Sunday

95

5 例にならって、日本語と英語を結ぼう。

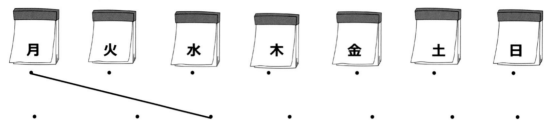

| 月 | 火 | 水 | 木 | 金 | 土 | 日 |

Wednesday   Saturday   Monday   Thursday   Sunday   Tuesday   Friday

6 月曜日から順に並^{なら}べかえて、番号で答えよう。

___ → ___ → ___ → ___ → ___ → ___ → ___

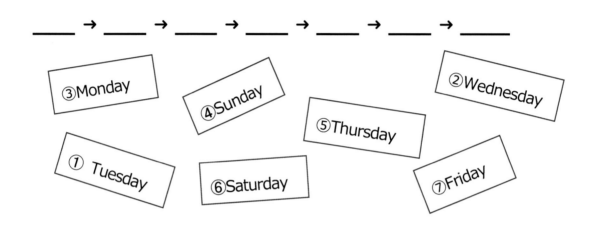

③Monday
④Sunday
②Wednesday
⑤Thursday
①Tuesday
⑥Saturday
⑦Friday

7 月曜日から日曜日まで順になるように、___ にアルファベットを入れよう。

1. M ___ n d ___ y

2. T ___ ___ s d a y

3. W ___ d n ___ s d a y

4. T h ___ r s d ___ y

5. F r ___ d ___ y

6. S ___ t ___ r d a y

7. S ___ n d ___ y

96

8 例にならって、今日の曜日を答えるやりとりを練習しよう。

 What day is it today?   It's Wednesday.

1. **What day is it today?**   - It's _____.   火曜日です。

2. **What _____ is it today?**   - It's _____.   金曜日です。

3. **_____ _____ is it today?**   - It's _____.   日曜日です。

4. **What day ___ ___ today?**   - It's _____.   月曜日です。

5. **_____ day ___ it _____?**   - ___ _____.   土曜日です。

6. **_____ _____ ___ ___ _____?** - ___ _____.   木曜日です。

大問9

9 よく聞いて時間の言い方を練習しよう。

1. It's three.   2. It's six.   3. It's nine.   4. It's eleven.

大問10

10 聞こえてきた順に番号をつけよう。

1.

( )   (1)   ( )   ( )   ( )

2.

( )   ( )   ( )   ( )   ( )

97

11 時間をたずねるやりとりを練習しよう。

 What time is it now?　　　　It's <u>ten</u> .

1. What time is it now?

   - It's _____ .

2. What time _____ _____ now?

   - It's seven.

3. _____ _____ is it now?

   - It's _____ .

4. What time is it now?

   - It's _____ .

4. には自由に時間を書こう。

大問１２

12 よく聞いて、くりかえし言おう。

What time is it, Mom?

It's eight o'clock.
　　　　　　時

Eight o'clock?

I'm late for school, Mom!
　ちこく する 学 校

What day is it today?

Oh, it's Sunday!

No school today!

98

Key Points　英語、日本語の順に声に出して読んでみよう。

What day is it today?		What time is it now?	
今日は何曜日ですか。		今、何時ですか。	
- It's ….	…曜日です。	- It's … .	…時です。
- It's Monday.	月曜日です。	- It's 10.	10 時です。

13 英語をなぞろう。

What time is it now?

It's twelve.

14 ＿＿＿＿ に英語を入れて、時間の聞き方と答え方を完成させよう。

1.

＿＿＿＿＿ ＿＿＿＿＿ ＿＿＿＿ ＿＿＿＿ ＿＿＿＿ ?　　　今、何時ですか。

2. ＿＿＿＿＿＿ **seven.**

3. **It's** ＿＿＿＿＿＿＿＿.

4. ＿＿＿＿＿＿ ＿＿＿＿＿＿＿＿.

5. ＿＿＿＿＿＿ ＿＿＿＿＿＿＿.

5. には自由に時間を書こう。

now　What　time　it

It's　three　five　is

99

EXTRA (UNIT 11 - UNIT 13)

1 知っている単語を○で囲もう。

Sunday fatherbedkitchengardentableThursday

2 Ana は何をたずねているのだろう。家族、家具、部屋、曜日、文ぼう具に関する単語を消していき、残った単語を並べかえて質問を作ろう。

Tuesday	a ruler	your father	a pencil case
a living room	Friday	Is	a sofa
your friend	a sister	a notebook	a big brother
a pen	Monday	a kitchen	she
a bed	a chair	a desk	Saturday

_____ _____ _____?

3 の中に下から英語を選んで入れよう。

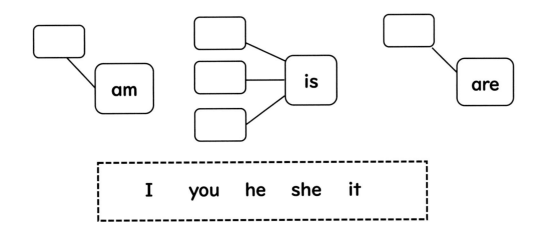

```
[    ]
       am

[    ]
[    ]      is
[    ]

[    ]
       are
```

```
┌ ─ ─ ─ ─ ─ ─ ─ ─ ─ ─ ─ ─ ─ ─ ─ ┐
      I    you   he   she   it
└ ─ ─ ─ ─ ─ ─ ─ ─ ─ ─ ─ ─ ─ ─ ─ ┘
```

4 例にならって、サイコロを2回ふって、出た目の数の英語を言おう。

1回目　2回目

例)　⚀　⚂　= I am hungry.

⚀ I am	⚀ kind.
⚁ You are	⚁ happy.
⚂ He is	⚂ hungry.
⚃ She is	**+** ⚃ good.
⚄ My teacher is	⚄ old.
⚅ Your teachers are	⚅ young.

101

5 順番に時間を言おう。2分以内、1分以内、30秒以内で言おう。

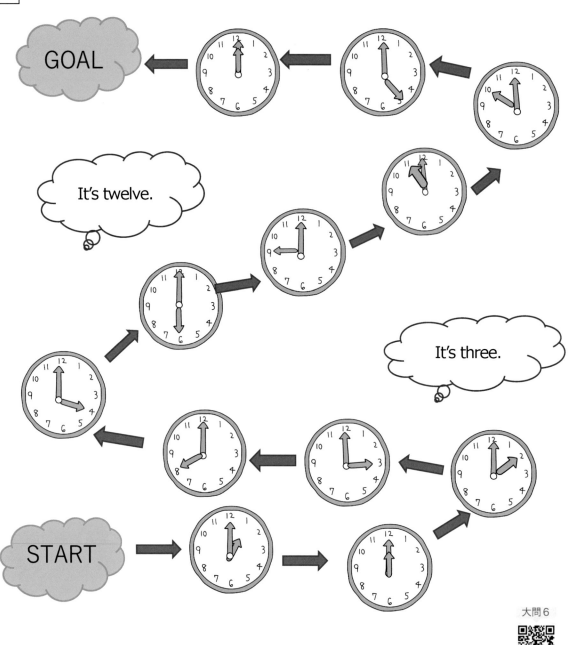

It's twelve.

It's three.

GOAL

START

大問6

6 英語を聞いて、英語の質問に対する正しい答えを選び、□ にアルファベットを書こう。

1. What time is it now? □

2. Where is Tom? □

3. Do you like bananas? □

4. Where are you from? □

5. Who are you? □

A. In the living room.

B. It's ten.

C. Yes, I do.

D. I'm Alice.

E. I'm from Kobe.

102

7 イラストにあう正しい方の英語を選ぼう。

1. It is | Wednesday | / | Thursday |.

2. It is | ten | / | eleven | .

3. He is | Pam | / | Kenta | .

4. The bag is | big | / | small | .

5. | Three | / | Five | books are in the bag.

8 例にならって、正しい順番になるよう(   )に番号を入れよう。

例) your – name – What's – ?

　　（ 2 ）（ 3 ）　（ 1 ）

1. is – My father – tall – .

　　(   )   (   )   (   )

2. she – Where – is – ?

　　(   )   (   )   (   )

3. it – What time – is – now – ?

　　(   )   (   )   (   ) (   )

4. It – seven – is – .

　　(   )   (   )   (   )

5. What day – today – it – is – ?

　　(   )   (   ) (   ) (   )

103

9 例にならって、3つの □ A B C の中の英語をつないで、文を作ろう。

例) She is in the garden.   /   Mr. Nakamura is tall.

A	B	C
I		happy.
You		hungry.
He		kind.
She	am	big.
Ichiro	are	tall.
Naomi	is	nine.
My friend		ten.
My father		in the kitchen.
My mother		in the garden.
Mr. _____		from Japan.
Ms. _____		from The USA.

Mr. _____ Ms. _____ には自分の先生の名前を入れよう。

作った英文を一つ選び、書こう。

_____

_____

104

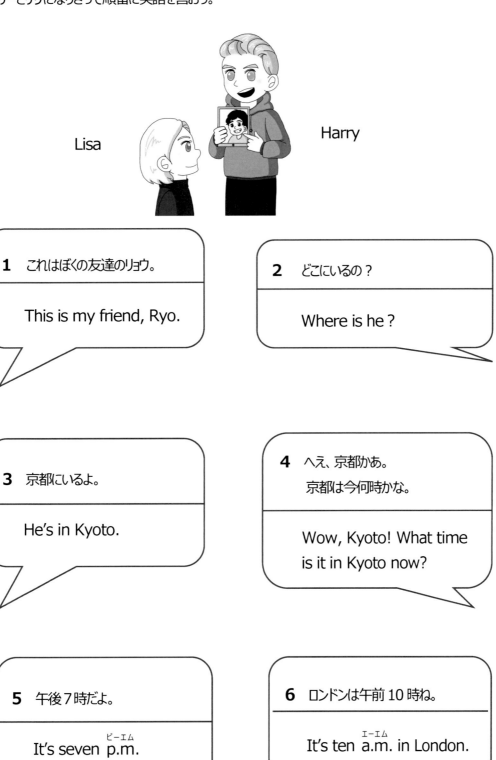

Lisa

Harry

1 これはぼくの友達のリョウ。

This is my friend, Ryo.

2 どこにいるの？

Where is he ?

3 京都にいるよ。

He's in Kyoto.

4 へえ、京都かあ。
京都は今何時かな。

Wow, Kyoto! What time
is it in Kyoto now?

5 午後7時だよ。

It's seven p.m.
^{ピーエム}

6 ロンドンは午前10時ね。

It's ten a.m. in London.
^{エーエム}

11 Lucy からのメッセージを聞いて、質問に答えよう。

Hi! How are you?

I'm in London. It's Sunday morning. It's ten.

What day is it and what time is it in Japan?

I have a friend. His name is George. He is from the U.K.

My teacher is kind. She is from the USA.

Lucy

Send

＊send　送信

1．①〜④の文が Lucy のメッセージの内容にあっていれば○を、間違っていれば□に×を入れよう。

① ルーシーは今ロンドンにいる。　□

② ルーシーは日曜日の朝にメールを書いている。　□

③ ルーシーの友達はアメリカ出身である。　□

④ ルーシーの先生は男の先生である。　□

2．ロンドンが日曜日の午前 10 時なら日本は何曜日の何時になるだろう。あてはまる曜日に○をつけ、時計に針を書こう。

Saturday　　　Sunday　　　Monday

UNIT 14

Target Sentences

How many desks?	机<ruby>つくえ</ruby>はいくつありますか。
- Fifteen.	－ 15 あります。
- Thirty-one.	－ 31 あります。

1 よく聞いて、くりかえし言おう。

thirteen	13
fourteen	14
fifteen	15
sixteen	16
seventeen	17
eighteen	18
nineteen	19
twenty	20
twenty-one	21
thirty	30
forty	40
fifty	50

2 よく聞いて、聞こえた方の数字に〇をつけよう。

1. 15 / 50   2. 13 / 30   3. 8 / 18   4. 7 / 17

5. 9 / 19   6. 12 / 20   7. 20 / 21   8. 14 / 40

3 よく聞いて、くりかえし言おう。

21	**22**	**23**	**24**	**25**
twenty-one	twenty-two	twenty-three	twenty-four	twenty-five
26	**27**	**28**	**29**	**30**
twenty-six	twenty-seven	twenty-eight	twenty-nine	thirty
35	**40**	**45**	**50**	
thirty-five	forty	forty-five	fifty	

4 小さい数から順番に並んでいるものを3つの中から選んで、☐ に✔を入れよう。

1. ・ two → five → three → one → four ☐
   ・ three → four → one → five → two ☐
   ・ one → two → three → four → five ☐

2. ・ fifteen → thirteen → sixteen → fourteen ☐
   ・ thirteen → fourteen → fifteen → sixteen ☐
   ・ sixteen → fifteen → fourteen → thirteen ☐

5 英語の表す数字を書こう。

1. sixteen _____
2. twenty _____
3. twenty-four _____

4. thirty-three _____
5. forty _____
6. thirteen _____

7. fifteen _____
8. eighteen _____
9. fifty _____

108

6 例にならって、聞こえた順に数字をたどっていって会えた人物を答えよう。

例) 10 → 15 → 31 → 48 → 40 ___Emily___

		28	10	25		
	41	20	50	15 → 31		
21	12	33	47	27	48	11
26	46	13	15	18	29	40
Mr.Green	Fred	Alice	Ms.Brown	Kenta	Ana	Emily

1. _____

2. _____

3. _____

7 計算した答えを数字で書いて、英語で言おう。

例) ten + one = 11

1. seven + eight= _____

2. nine + four= _____

3. twelve + five = _____

4. twenty-one + one=_____

5. twenty-six + three = _____

6. thirty − two = _____

7. forty-eight − two =_____

8. forty − ten = _____

9. thirty − sixteen = _____

10. fifty − eleven = _____

8 よく聞いて、質問文(しつもんぶん)と答えをくりかえし言おう。次に Mike, Ms. Sasaki, Mr. Green, Ms. Brown, Mr. Ito になりきって、質問(しつもん)に答えよう。

> How old are you, Kaito?

> I'm eleven.

1.　　　　　2.　　　　　3.　　　　　4.　　　　　5.

Mike(18才)　Ms. Sasaki(24才)　Mr. Green(32才)　Ms. Brown(40才)　Mr. Ito(50才)

9 よく聞いて、くりかえし言おう。

Let's count down!

Twenty, nineteen, eighteen, seventeen,

sixteen, fifteen, fourteen, thirteen,

twelve, eleven, ten!

Good job!

Again, faster!

＊count down: 逆(ぎゃく)にかぞえる

＊faster: もっとはやく

Key Points 英語、日本語の順に声に出して読んでみよう。

How many＿＿＿＿s ?	…はいくつありますか。
How many apples?	りんごはいくつありますか。
-　Five.	－5こあります。
-　Fifteen.	－15こあります。
-　Fifty.	－50こあります。

110

10 絵を見て、果物や野菜の数と数字を結ぼう。

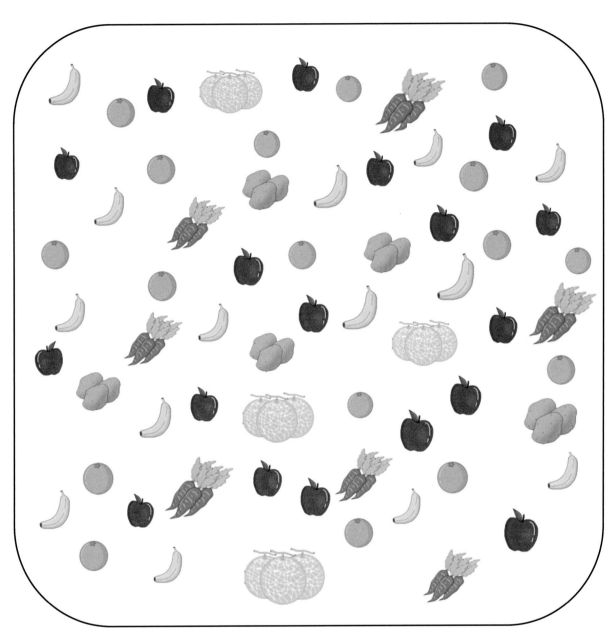

How many?

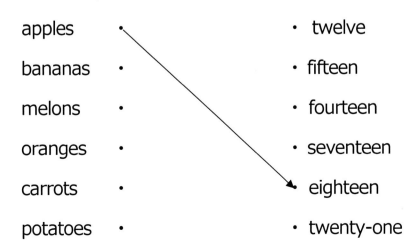

apples ·   · twelve

bananas ·   · fifteen

melons ·   · fourteen

oranges ·   · seventeen

carrots ·   · eighteen

potatoes ·   · twenty-one

11 次の質問に英語で答えよう。

1. How many students in your class? _____

2. How many teachers in your school? _____

3. How many pencils in your pencil case? _____

4. How many desks in your classroom? _____

5. How many bags in your classroom? _____

12 英語をなぞろう。

thirteen   fourteen   fifteen

sixteen   seventeen   eighteen

nineteen   twenty   twenty-one

thirty   forty   fifty

UNIT 15

Target Sentences

> Go straight. 　　　　まっすぐに進みなさい。
>
> Turn right. 　　　　右に曲がりなさい。
>
> Don't turn left. 　　左に曲がってはいけません。

1 よく聞いて、くりかえし言おう。

go	行く
straight	まっすぐに
turn	向きを変える
right	右
left	左
turn right	右に曲がる
turn left	左に曲がる
walk	歩く
stop	止まる
read	読む
write	書く
homework	宿題
do 〜homework	宿題をする

2 よく聞いて、くりかえし言おう。

| Turn left. | Turn right. | Go straight. | Stop. |

3 英語にあうイラストを選び □ にアルファベットを書こう。

1. run □
2. read □
3. write □
4. jump □
5. sing □
6. walk □
7. swim □
8. ride a bicycle □
9. play soccer □
10. play the recorder □

A   B   C

D   E   F

G   H

I   J

114

4 下から英語を選び、その動作をしよう。

run	turn right	turn left	walk
sing	write	read	stop

大問5

5 よく聞いて、くりかえし言おう。

Run fast!（速く）   — OK!

Dance well!   — Sure!（りょうかい）

Jump high!   — All right!!（りょうかい）

Do your homework!   — No, way!（いやだ）

Do your Homework!

6 例にならって、Alice がスピーカーで言いたいことを英語で言おう。

例)

Run.

115

Key Points 英語、日本語の順に声に出して読んでみよう。

Go straight. まっすぐに進みなさい。	**Don't** run. 走ってはいけません。
Turn right. 右に曲がりなさい。	**Don't** stop. 止まってはいけません。

7 下から文を選んで、Don't の文にして言おう。

例)　Run.　→ **Don't** run.

　　　Jump.　→ **Don't** jump.

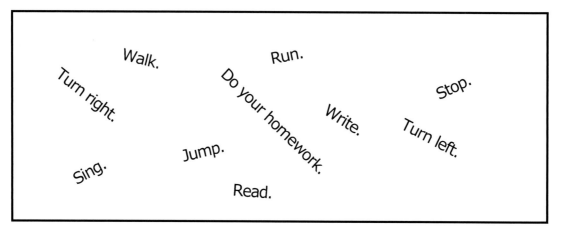

8 例にならって、サイコロを2つふろう。出た目の合計数の英語を言おう。

③Don't turn right.

② Sing.　　　　　⑧ Turn right.

③ Don't turn right.　⑨ Go straight.

④ Stop.　　　　　⑩ Turn left.

⑤ Don't run.　　　⑪ Don't sing.

⑥ Read.　　　　　⑫ Walk.

⑦ Don't jump.

9 例にならって、次のサインは何を表しているか考えて、英語と結ぼう。

1. ・

     ・ Turn left.

2. ・

     ・ Walk

3. ・

     ・ Don't write.

4. ・

     ・ Stop.

5. ・

     ・ Go straight.

6. ・

     ・ Don't swim.

10 あなたの先生になりきって、イラストにあうように「～しなさい」「～してはいけません」と言おう。

1. 2. 3. 4.

11 英語をなぞろう。

Run.　Don't run.

Sing.　Don't sing.

UNIT 16

Target Sentences

Do you get up at six?	あなたは 6 時に起きますか。
- No, I don't.	- いいえ、起きません。
What time do you get up?	何時に起きますか。
- I get up at seven.	- 7 時に起きます。
- I get up at seven ten.	- 7 時 10 分に起きます。

1 よく聞いて、くりかえし言おう。

get up	起きる
bed	ベッド
go to bed	寝る
eat	食べる
breakfast	朝食
lunch	昼食
dinner	夕食
bath	お風呂
take a bath	お風呂にはいる
watch TV	テレビを見る
study	勉強する
at school	学校で
at home	家で
a.m.	午前
p.m.	午後

2 聞こえてきた順番を数字で書こう。

( )　　( )　　( )　　( )　　( )

3 英語にあうイラストを選び、記号を書こう。

1. take a bath　□
2. go to bed　□
3. study　□
4. watch TV　□
5. eat breakfast　□

A

B

C

D

E

4 それぞれの時間帯に行う英語を選んで □ に番号を書こう。

12:00

a.m.

p.m.

At school

6:00

6:00

At home

a.m.

p.m.

12:00

1. get up	2. go to bed	3. eat breakfast	4. eat lunch
5. eat dinner	6. study	7. watch TV	8. take a bath

5 よく聞いて、次の質問に対する自分の答えを〇で囲もう。

大問5

1. Do you eat breakfast at seven?   - Yes, I do. / No, I don't.

2. Do you eat lunch at school?   - Yes, I do. / No, I don't.

3. Do you watch TV at school?   - Yes, I do. / No, I don't.

4. Do you study at home?   - Yes, I do. / No, I don't.

5. Do you get up at six?   - Yes, I do. / No, I don't.

6. Do you go to bed at ten?   - Yes, I do. / No, I don't.

6 よく聞いて、くりかえし言おう。

大問6

1. What time do you get up?   - At six.

2. What time do you eat breakfast?   - At seven.

3. What time do you eat lunch?   - At twelve.

4. What time do you study?   - At five.

5. What time do you eat dinner?   - At six.

6. What time do you watch TV?   - At eight.

7. What time do you take a bath?   - At nine.

大問7

7 よく聞いて、くりかえし言おう。

1. `6 : 10` It's six ten.　I get up at six ten.

2. `7 : 15` It's seven fifteen.　I eat breakfast at seven fifteen.

3. `12 : 30` It's twelve thirty.　I eat lunch at twelve thirty.

4. `8 : 45` It's eight forty-five.　I take a bath at eight forty-five.

5. `9 : 50` It's nine fifty.　I go to bed at nine fifty.

8 よく聞いて、それぞれの先生の起きる時間を線で結ぼう。

1. Ms. Brown   2. Mr. Green   3. Ms. Sasaki

| 5:30 | 6:00 | 6:30 | 7:00 |

9 よく聞いて、くりかえし言おう。

What time?　What time?

What time do you get up?

　At six.

　At six.

　I get up at six.

Oh, you are an early^{朝 が た} bird.

What time?　What time?

What time do you go to bed?

　At twelve.

　At twelve.

　I go to bed at twelve.

Oh, you are a night^{夜 が た} owl.

121

Key Points　英語、日本語の順に声に出して読んでみよう。

Do you get up at seven? あなたは 7 時に起きますか。	Yes, I do. / No, I don't. はい、起きます。/ いいえ、起きません。
What time do you …? あなたは何時に…しますか。	What time do you get up? あなたは何時に起きますか。
I … at ～ . わたしは～時に…をします。	I get up at six. わたしは 6 時に起きます。

10　例にならって、英語を組みあわせ、できるだけたくさん文を作ってみよう。

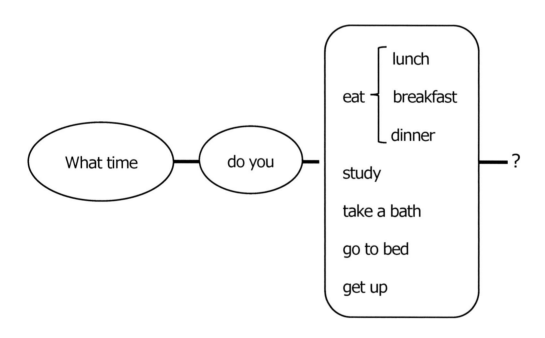

例)

What time do you eat lunch?

122

11 よく聞いて、質問文と答えをくりかえし言おう。次に Alice, Jack, Fred になりきって、質問に答えよう。

例)

What time do you get up?

I get up at six ten.

	1.	2.	3.
get up	7:00	6:30	7:15
eat breakfast	7:30	7:15	7:40
eat dinner	6:00	6:10	8:00
take a bath	8:20	7:40	9:30
go to bed	10:00	9:50	11:00

12 英語をなぞろう。

What time do you get up?

I get up at seven.

Do you eat lunch at twelve?

What time do you study?

13 例にならって、正しい順番になるよう( )に番号を入れよう。

例) your – name – What's – ?
(2) (3)　　(1)

1. get up –　you – What time –　do – ?
( )　　( )　　( )　　　( )

2. get　– I　–　up – at seven　– .
( )　( )　( )　( )

3. Do　–　eat lunch –　you　– at twelve –?
( )　　　( )　　　( )　　( )

4. time　–　do you –　What　–　study　– ?
( )　　　( )　　　( )　　　( )

EXTRA (UNIT 14 – UNIT 16)

1 A、B、C、D の中で種類のちがう英語に〇をつけよう。

1.

A. eight
B. twenty
C. thirty
D. forty

2.

A. read
B. write
C. white
D. study

3.

A. lunch
B. dinner
C. eat
D. breakfast

2 左の英語に続けて、あてはまる英語を言おう。

1. thirteen, fourteen, fifteen, _____

2. twenty-one, twenty-two, twenty-three _____

3. ten, twenty, thirty, _____

4. at two, at two thirty, at three, _____

5. at one fifteen, at one forty-five, at two fifteen, _____

3 例にならって、意味が通るように、左の英語と右の英語を結びつけよう。

1. eat   • bed

2. take   •   • breakfast

3. watch   •   • a bath

4. turn   •   • TV

5. go to   •   • right

4 例にならって、下線部に時間を書こう。次に声に出して英語を読もう。

例)

6:00　I get up <u>at six</u>.

1. 7:00　I eat breakfast _____.

2. 8:00　I go to school _____.

3. 12:00　I eat lunch _____.

4. 4:00　I study at home _____.

5. 5:00　I play soccer _____.

大問5

5 英語の質問を聞いて、その答えを選び、アルファベットで答えよう。

1. How many apples? ☐ 　　2. What time do you take a bath? ☐

3. What day is it today? ☐ 　　4. Do you get up at seven? ☐

A. It's Thursday.

B. At eight

C. Fifteen.

D. Yes, I do.

126

6 下から英語を選び、その動作をしよう。

Sing.   Walk.   Dance.   Jump.
Turn right.   Go straight.
Run.   Turn left.   Stop.

7 お医者さんがカゼをひいた患者さんに言うアドバイスを考えよう。例にならって、Aの◯の中の英語とBの◯の中の英語をつなごう。

〜しなさい
例) Eat apples.

〜してはいけません。
Don't take a bath.

_____

_____

_____

_____

_____

_____

_____

_____

A

eat

go

take

play

B

to bed at eight.

to school.

apples.

a bath.

breakfast.

soccer.

bananas.

dodgeball.

❀ 他のアドバイスを考えて言おう。

8 あなたは友達の Jack に質問をしています。Jack の英語が答えとなる質問を A～E から選んで、
＿＿＿ にアルファベットを書こう。

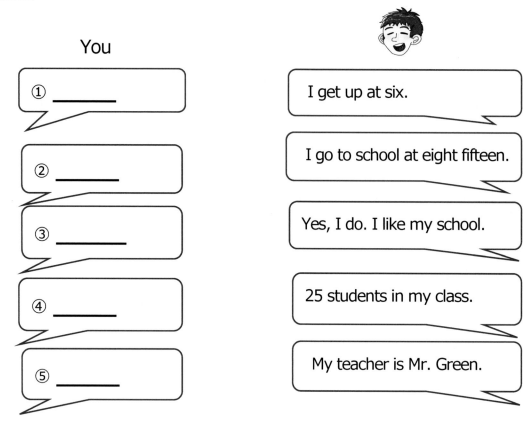

You

① ＿＿＿＿＿

② ＿＿＿＿＿

③ ＿＿＿＿＿

④ ＿＿＿＿＿

⑤ ＿＿＿＿＿

I get up at six.

I go to school at eight fifteen.

Yes, I do. I like my school.

25 students in my class.

My teacher is Mr. Green.

A.　Who is your teacher?

B.　Do you like your school?

C.　What time do you get up?

D.　What time do you go to school?

E.　How many students in your class?

9 Emily が夏休みにあなたの家にやってきました。英語を聞き例にならって、Emily の質問に答えよう。

あなたの似顔絵

What time do you get up?

例：At six.

What time do you eat breakfast?

What time do you eat lunch?

What time do you go home?

What time do you eat dinner?

What time do you go to bed?

129

UNIT 17

Target Sentences

> Where do you want to go? あなたはどこに行きたいですか。
>
>   - I want to go to the zoo. － 動物園に行きたいです。
>
>   - I want to go to Canada. － カナダに行きたいです。

1 よく聞いて、くりかえして言おう。

大問1

a **zoo**	動物園
a **park**	公園
a **library**	図書館
an **aquarium**	水族館
a **movie theater**	映画館
a **swimming pool**	プール
Canada	カナダ
France	フランス
Germany	ドイツ
Vietnam	ベトナム
Finland	フィンランド
South Africa	南アフリカ

2 日本語にあう英語を選んで、____ に番号を書こう。

1. 公園 _____

2. 動物園 _____

3. 映画館 _____

4. 図書館 _____

5. プール _____

6. 水族館 _____

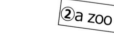

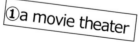
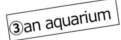

130

3 聞こえてきた順に番号をつけよう。

1.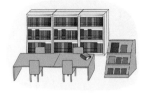

( ) ( ) ( )

2.

( ) ( ) ( )

4 例にならって、I want to go to「〜に行きたい」の文にして、言おう。

例) **I want to go to the aquarium.** 水族館に行きたい。

1. **I want to go to the _____.** 公園に行きたい。

2. **I want to ____ to the _____.** 図書館に行きたい。

3. **I want to ____ ____ the _____.** 動物園に行きたい。

4. **I ____ to ____ ____ the swimming_____.** プールに行きたい。

5. **I _____ ___ __ ____ the _____theater.** 映画館に行きたい。

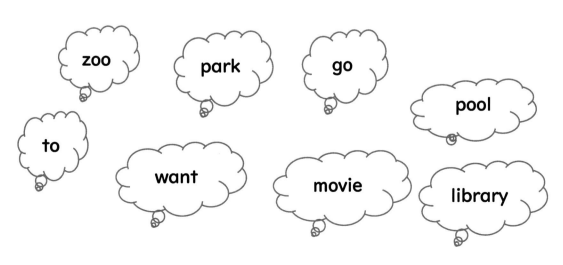

zoo park go

pool

to

want movie library

5 聞こえてきた順に番号をつけよう。

南アフリカ　　　　ドイツ　　　　フランス　　　　ベトナム　　　フィンランド

（　　）　　　（　　）　　　　（　　）　　　（　　）　　　（　　）

6 国名を下から選んで、⬜ に番号を書こう。次に国の名前を英語で言おう。

Korea　①

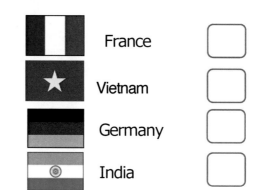

France　⬜

South Africa　⬜

Vietnam　⬜

Canada　⬜

Germany　⬜

China　⬜

India　⬜

①韓国（かんこく）　　②ドイツ　　③中国　　④南アフリカ

⑤ベトナム　　⑥フランス　　⑦インド　　⑧カナダ

7 次の単語の＿＿にアルファベットを入れよう。

1. F ＿ n l ＿ n d
2. I n d ＿ ＿
3. F r ＿ n c ＿
4. G ＿ r m ＿ n y
5. V ＿ e t n ＿ m

a　　e

i　　o

132

8 サイコロの目の数だけ進んだら、そのコマの国名を言おう。

START

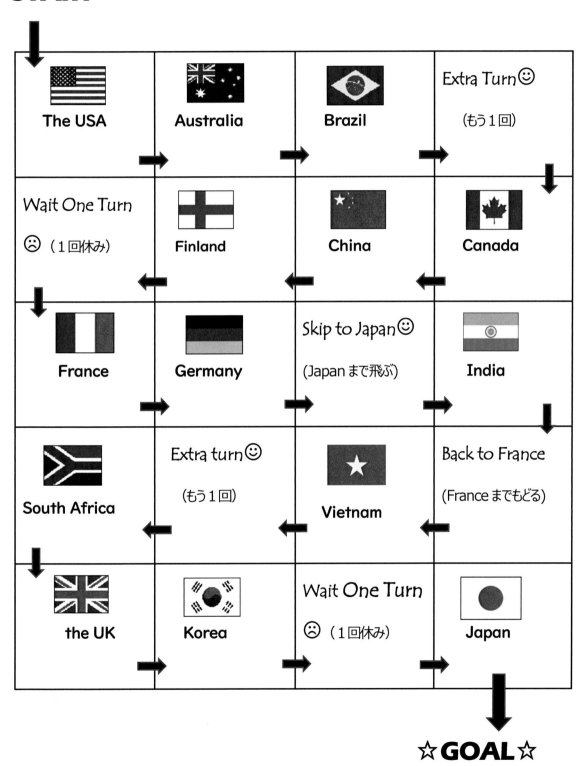

The USA	Australia	Brazil	Extra Turn☺ (もう1回)
Wait One Turn ☹（1回休み）	Finland	China	Canada
France	Germany	Skip to Japan☺ (Japanまで飛ぶ)	India
South Africa	Extra turn☺ （もう1回）	Vietnam	Back to France (Franceまでもどる)
the UK	Korea	Wait One Turn ☹（1回休み）	Japan

☆GOAL☆

9 「どこへ行きたいですか？」を練習しよう。_____に英語を入れて、言おう。

> **Where do you want to go?**

1. **Where do you want to _____?**

2. **Where _____ _____ want to _____?**

3. **Where _____ _____ _____ to _____?**

4. **_____ _____ _____ want _____ go?**

5. **_____ do you _____ _____ _____?**

大問10

10 よく聞いて、くりかえし言おう。

Where do you want to go, Fred?

I want to go to the swimming pool.

I like swimming.

あ な た は ど う
How about you, Kenta?

I want to go to the movie theater.

I like movies.

Where do you want to go, Alice?

I want to go to the movie theater too.

Let's go together!

Yes, let's!

11 よく聞いて、質問文と答えをくりかえして言おう。次に Kenta, Alice, Lucy, Ana になりきって、質問に答えよう。

Where do you want to go?

I want to go to the park.

1

2

3

4

Key Points　英語、日本語の順に声に出して読んでみよう。

Where do you want to go?	I want to go to Canada.
あなたはどこへ行きたいですか。	わたしはカナダに行きたいです。

135

12 英語をなぞろう。

Where do you want to go?

I want to go to Canada.

I want to go to the park.

13 例にならって、正しい順番になるよう( )に番号を入れよう。

例) your – name – What's – ?
（２）（３）（１）

1. want to – the park – I – go to – .
（ ） （ ） （ ） （ ）

2. do you – Where – go – want to – ?
（ ） （ ） （ ） （ ）

3. to Canada – want – to go – I – .
（ ） （ ） （ ） （ ）

UNIT 18

Target Sentences

> When is your birthday?　　　　　　あなたの誕生日_{たんじょうび}はいつですか。
>
> - My birthday is February 14th.　　 － ２月１４日です。

1 よく聞いて、くりかえし言おう。

大問１

January	1月
February	2月
March	3月
April	4月
May	5月
June	6月
July	7月
August	8月
September	9月
October	10月
November	11月
December	12月

137

2 うすい字をなぞって、月の名前にしよう。

1.	1月	January	January
2.	2月	February	February
3.	3月	March	March
4.	4月	April	April
5.	5月	May	May
6.	6月	June	June
7.	7月	July	July
8.	8月	August	August
9.	9月	September	September
10.	10月	October	October
11.	11月	November	November
12.	12月	December	December

3 例にならって、日本語と英語を結ぼう。

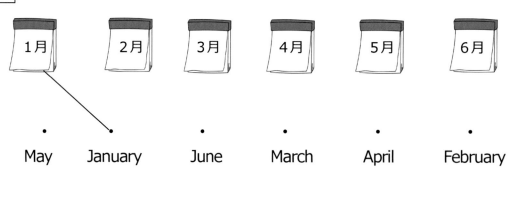

1月　2月　3月　4月　5月　6月

May　January　June　March　April　February

7月　8月　9月　10月　11月　12月

September　December　October　August　July　November

138

4 早い月から順番にならべかえて、番号で答えよう。

<u>　②　</u> → <u>　　　</u> → <u>　　　</u> → <u>　　　</u> → <u>　　　</u> → <u>　　　</u> → <u>　　　</u>

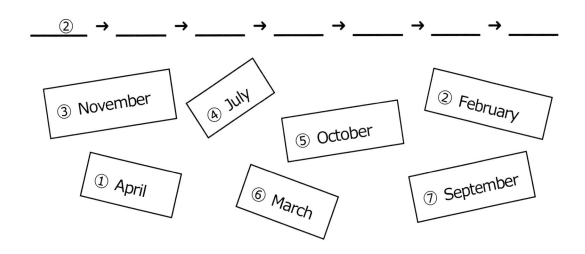

③ November

④ July

⑤ October

② February

① April

⑥ March

⑦ September

✻ぬけている月を言おう

5 空白の場所にアルファベットを入れて、月の名前を完成しよう。

J		n			r	y		
F		b	r			r	y	
M		r	c	h				
A	p	r		l				
M		y						
J		n						
J		l	y					
A		g		s	t			
S		p	t		m	b		r
O	c	t		b		r		
N		v		m	b		r	
D		c		m	b		r	

a
e
i
o
u

139

6 聞こえてきた順に番号をつけよう。

1. January   February   March   April

 (   )   (   )   (   )   (   )

2. May   June   July   August

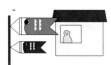    

 (   )   (   )   (   )   (   )

3. September October November December

 (   )   (   )   (   )   (   )

7 聞こえてきた月の名前を○で囲もう。

1.	January	February	March
2.	April	May	June
3.	July	August	September
4.	October	November	December
5.	May	July	March
6.	September	August	October
7.	January	February	July

Key Points　英語、日本語の順に声に出して読んでみよう。

When is your birthday? あなたの誕生日はいつですか。	- My birthday is February 14th. 2月14日です。
(the) 1st	(the) **first**
(the) 2nd	(the) **second**
(the) 3rd	(the) **third**
(the) 4th	(the) fourth
(the) 5th	(the) **fif**th
(the) 6th	(the) sixth
(the) 7th	(the) seventh
(the) 8th	(the) **eigh**th
(the) 9th	(the) **nin**th
(the) 10th	(the) tenth
(the) 11th	(the) eleventh
(the) 12th	(the) **twelf**th
(the) 13th	(the) thirteenth
(the) 14th	(the) fourteenth
(the) 15th	(the) fifteenth
(the) 16th	(the) sixteenth
(the) 17th	(the) seventeenth
(the) 18th	(the) eighteenth
(the) 19th	(the) nineteenth
(the) 20th	(the) twent**ie**th
(the) 21st	(the) twenty-**first**
(the) 22nd	(the) twenty-**second**
(the) 23rd	(the) twenty-**third**
(the) 24th	(the) twenty-fourth
(the) 25th	(the) twenty-fifth
(the) 26th	(the) twenty-sixth
(the) 27th	(the) twenty-seventh
(the) 28th	(the) twenty-eighth
(the) 29th	(the) twenty-ninth
(the) 30th	(the) thirt**ie**th
(the) 31st	(the) thirty-**first**

8 よく聞いて、くりかえし言おう。

First, Second, Third, Fourth, Fifth.

　Go first.　Go second.　Go third.

　　Go fourth.　Go fifth.

Sixth, Seventh, Eighth, Ninth, Tenth.

　Go sixth.　Go seventh.　Go eighth.

　Go ninth.　Go tenth.

9 例にならって、左と右を結びつけよう。

4th ·		· first
1st ·		· eighth
5th ·		· tenth
8th ·		· third
2nd ·		· fourth
10th ·		· twelfth
3rd ·		· second
11th ·		· eleventh
12th ·		· fifth

10 例にならって、＿＿に st, nd, rd, th のいずれかを入れよう。

1.　3 rd　　　　2.　7＿＿＿　　　3.　1＿＿＿

4.　11＿＿＿　　5.　21＿＿＿　　6.　8＿＿＿

7.　9＿＿＿　　8.　2＿＿＿　　　9.　16＿＿＿

10.　23＿＿＿　　11.　22＿＿＿　　12.　5＿＿＿

11 1番目〜15番目まで順につなごう。

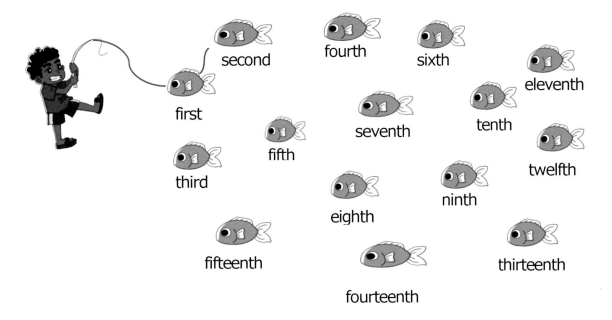

12 英語をなぞろう。

When is your birthday? – It's March 2nd.

When is your birthday? – It's April 3rd.

13 自分の生まれた誕生日を言おう。

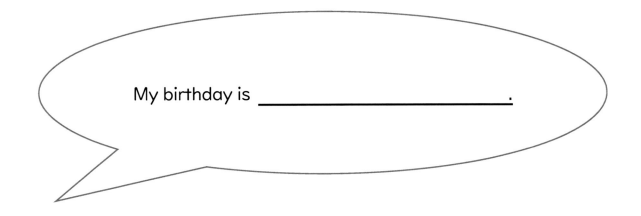

My birthday is _____.

サイコロゲームをしよう。順番にサイコロをふって、出た目の数だけ進み、その数字を言おう。

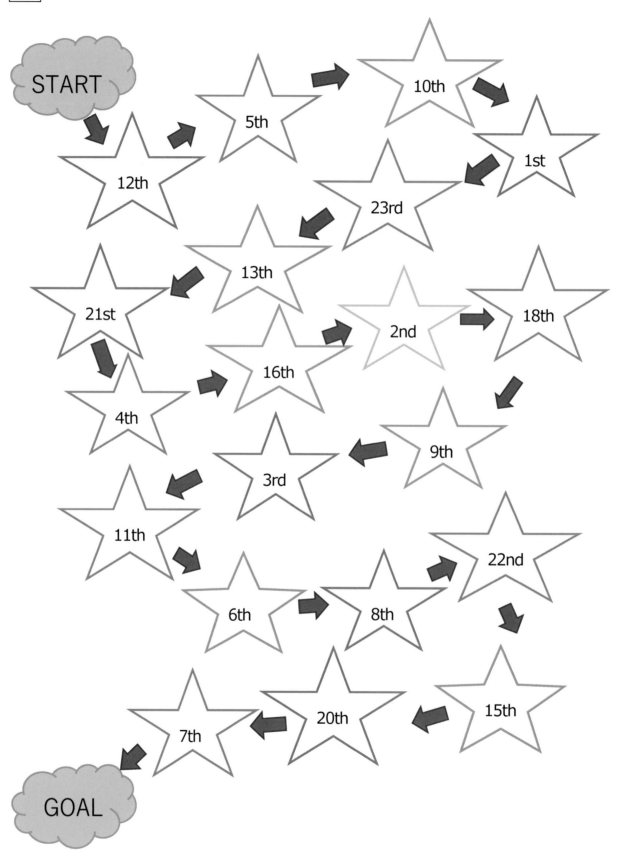

144

15 よく聞いて、質問文と答えをくりかえし言おう。次に Bill, Helen, Mari, Steve, Peter, Kate になりきって、質問に答えよう。

When is your birthday?

My birthday is January 7th

1
4月3日

2
6月8日

3
11月17日

Bill

Helen

Mari

4
10月10日

5
7月12日

6
5月1日

Steve

Peter

Kate

145

EXTRA (UNIT 17 – UNIT 18)

1 イラストをヒントに、空白部分にアルファベットを入れ、英語を完成しよう。

1		o	o								
2		a	r	k							
3		i	b	r	a	r					
4	a	q	u	a	r	i	u				
5		o	v	i	e		t	h	e	a	t	e	r
6	s	w	i		m	i	n	g		o	o	l

m z p l y

1.

2.

3.

4.

5.

6.

2 場所と関係のあるイラストのアルファベットを ☐ に書こう。

1. a movie theater [A]
2. a library [ ]
3. an aquarium [ ]
4. a park [ ]
5. a swimming pool [ ]
6. a zoo [ ]

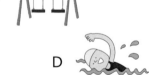

A

B

C

D

E

F

日本地図を見ながら、自分の行きたい場所ランキングを作ろう。

I want to go to …

順位	1st	2nd	3rd
都道府県（例）	Aomori	Nagasaki	Kagawa
都道府県（自分）			

例にならって、自分の行ききたいところを英語で言おう。

例）

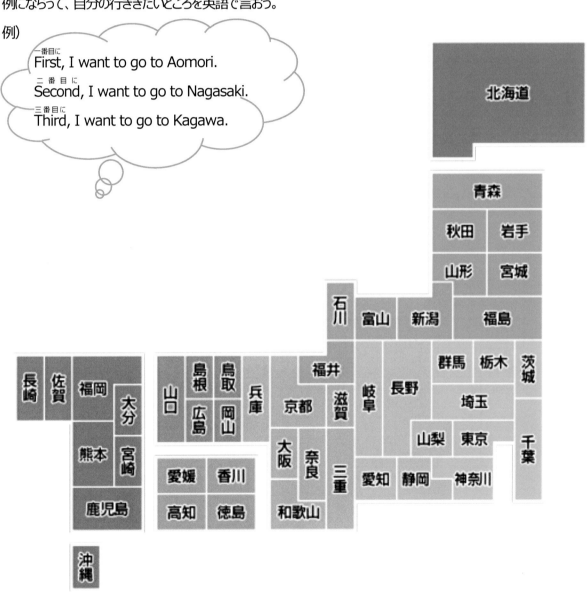

First, I want to go to Aomori.
Second, I want to go to Nagasaki.
Third, I want to go to Kagawa.

4 よく聞いて、Alice, Fred, Emily, Kenta の行きたい場所に ✓ をつけよう。

	Alice	Fred	Emily	Kenta

5 クロスワード。月の名前を大文字で完成しよう。水色のマスを上から読んで、HAPPY に続けて＿＿＿＿に書こう。

10月	O	C	T	O		E	R			
4月		A	P	R		L				
2月		F	E	B		U	A	R	Y	
9月		S	E	P		E	M	B	E	R
3月	M	A	R	C						
12月					E	C	E	M	B	E	R
1月		J		N	U	A	R	Y		
5月		M	A							

HAPPY ＿＿＿＿＿＿＿＿＿＿＿＿＿＿＿！

148

6 1番目(first)から8番目までを順に○で囲もう。

(first)secondthirdfourthfifthsixthseventheighth

7 例にならって、それぞれ何月をさすか考えて答えよう。

例) Christmas　　　　　　　→ ___December___ *month: 月
　　The 3rd month　　　　　→ ___March___

1. Valentine's Day　　　　　　_____

2. You can ski. (複数答えてもOK)　_____

3. You can swim. (複数答えてもOK)　_____

4. Your birthday　　　　　　_____

5. Your teacher's birthday　_____

6. The 1st month　　　　　_____

7. The 6th month　　　　　_____

8. The 11th month　　　　_____

January	February	March	April
May	June	July	August
September	October	November	December

149

8 次の1〜5の質問にあてはまる人物の名前を言おう。

1. Who is in the 2nd 場所 place? _____

2. Who is in the 8th place? _____

3. Who is in the 5th place? _____

4. Who is in the 10th place? _____

5. Who is in the 3rd place? _____

謝　辞

　本ワークブックの作成にあたり、フィンランド英語教育の先駆者である鳴門教育大学名誉教授伊東治己先生からは多くの示唆と助言を頂きました。深く感謝申し上げます。また、本ワークブックのなぞり書きのプラクティスは、高知大学多良静也先生が開発されたプログラム「英語習字印刷」を使わせていただきました。ご提供いただきましたことに深く感謝いたします。さらに、適切なご助言をいただきました清風堂書店の長谷川桃子様にも心から感謝いたします。

　皆様のご協力とご支援がなければ、本ワークブックの完成は実現しなかったことでしょう。心より御礼申し上げます。

著者紹介

米崎　里（よねざき　みち）

関西学院大学教育学部准教授。兵庫県教育大学大学院連合学校教育学研究科博士課程修了。学校教育学博士。フィンランドの旅行がきっかけで、現地の英語教育に深く感銘を受け、以後フィンランドの英語教育に関する研究を続けている。なかでも教育現場における実践的な指導方法や教材開発に焦点を当て、それを日本の英語教育に応用する可能性を探求している。著書に『フィンランド人はなぜ「学校教育」だけで英語が話せるのか』（亜紀書房）、『国際的に見た外国語教員の要請』（共著、東信堂）、『アウトプット重視の英語授業』（共著、教育出版）などがある。

岩﨑　幸子（いわさき　さちこ）

前帝塚山学院中学校・高等学校教諭・京田辺シュタイナー学校非常勤講師。1996年奈良教育大学大学院修士課程修了、2005年関西学院大学大学院言語コミュニケーション文化研究科前期課程修了。著書『アウトプット重視の英語授業』（共著、教育出版）。

川見　和子（かわみ　かずこ）

甲南女子中学校高等学校英語科教諭。1993年大阪大学文学部文学科英文専攻（英語学）卒業。1999年同志社大学神学研究科修了。神学修士。1993年より私立中学高校で教鞭をとる。

カバー・表紙・扉デザイン／クリエイティブ・コンセプト
江森　恵子

フィンランド式
小学英語ワークブック　初級

2024年7月31日　初版　第1刷発行

著　者　©米崎　里・岩﨑　幸子
　　　　川見　和子
イラスト　©前田　慎也・永尾　夏希
編　集　関西学院大学・教育学部
　　　　米崎研究室
発行者　面　屋　　洋
発行所　清　風　堂　書　店
〒530-0057　大阪市北区曽根崎2-11-16
TEL　06（6313）1390
FAX　06（6314）1600
振替　00920-6-119910

制作編集担当・長谷川桃子

印刷・㈱関西共同印刷所／製本・立花製本
ISBN978-4-86709-038-1　C6082

フィンランド式 小学英語 ワークブック 初級 解答

清風堂書店

UNIT 1

2 （ 3 ） （ 1 ） （ 2 ）
（音声）Good afternoon.   Good night.   Good morning.

3 1. おはようございます。 2. こんにちは。 3. さようなら。 4. やあ。 5. おやすみなさい。

5 1. Good morning, Ms. Brown.   2. Good afternoon, Mr. Green.

3. Good bye, <u>あなたの先生の名前.</u>
（音声）1. Good morning, class.   2. Good afternoon, everyone.   3. Good bye, class.

6 1. Hello! I'm <u>Jack</u>.   2. My name is <u>Alice</u>.   3. Hi! I'm <u>Fred</u>.

4. Hello! my name is <u>Emily</u>.

7 (goodbye) (morning) (night) (hello)

8 1. your   2. my   3. my   4. your

1 0 解答例）Who are you? → I'm Sachi.   →What's your name?   →My name is Emily. →
My name is Hiro.など

11 1. is   2. your   3. you   4. I   5. my

13 1. your   2. My   3. you   4. I'm

UNIT 2

2 （音声）1. Japan   2. China   3. Australia   4. the USA   5. Brazil   6. the UK

3 1. rea   2. tralia   3. pan   4. dia   5. zil

6 1. Emily → the USA   2. Jack → the UK   3. Ana → Brazil   4. Lin→ China
（音声）1. Where are you from, Emily? – I'm from the USA.
2. Where are you from, Jack? – The UK. I'm from the UK.
3. Ana, where are you from? -   I'm from Brazil.
4. Where are you from, Lin? – China. I'm from China.

7 解答例）Where are you from?   - I'm from the USA. など

UNIT 3

2 1. [3]→[5]→[7]→[2]   2. [11]→[9]→[12]→[10]
3. [4]→[6]→[1]→[8]
（音声）1. three → five → seven → two   2. eleven → nine → twelve → ten
3. four → six →one →eight

| 3 | two _2_ | six _6_ | three _3_ | eleven _11_ | eight _8_ |

3   two _2_   six _6_   three _3_   eleven _11_   eight _8_

twelve _12_   four _4_   nine _9_   five _5_   seven _7_

4 one- two – three – four – five – six - seven – eight – nine - ten – eleven – twelve

5 six cakes / seven doughnuts / nine cherries

6 1. 3 (three)   2. 7 (seven)   3. 9 (nine)   4. 8 (eight)

    5. 1 (one)   6. 4 (four)   7. 6 (six)   10. 10 (ten)

7 上段から **t**hree **tw**o **se**ven e**l**even fi**v**e **t**en   出てきた数字 12 (twelve)

9 Kenta 11,   Ana 10,   Jack 11,   Lucy 12

    (音声) How old are you, Kenta? - I'm eleven. / How old are you, Ana? - I'm ten.

        How old are you, Jack?   - I'm eleven, too. / How old are you Lucy? -I'm twelve.

12 1. How old   2. I'm

UNIT 4

2   4 → 1 → 2 → 5 →3   (音声) fine hungry sleepy happy tired

4 解答例) I'm tired. →I'm not tired. など

7 解答例) 1. Are you fine? - Yes, I am.   2. Are you sleepy? - No, I'm not. など

8 1. No, I'm not. I'm from the USA.   2. Yes, I am. I'm happy.

    3. No, I'm not. I'm not sleepy.   4. Yes, I am. I'm hungry.

    5. No, I'm not. I'm eleven.

10 1. not   2. I'm not   3. not   4. You're not

11 1. Are / not   2. you / am

EXTRA (UNIT 1-4)

1 (上から順番に) Hello (もしくは Hi)！ / My name is (自分の名前).What's your name?

    Nice to meet you, too.

2 Hi! I'm from the UK.   Hi! I'm from the USA.   Hi! I'm from Brazil.

👧 Hi! I'm from China.   👦 Hi! I'm from Australia.

3 | 1.   2.   3.   4.   5.   6.
🇯🇵   🇬🇧   🇧🇷   🇨🇳   🇰🇷   🇮🇳

5 | 1. py   2. ry   3. y   4. en   5. leven

6 | 1. I'm Kenta.   2. I'm fine. Thank you   3. No, I'm not.   4. I'm eleven.

7 | 1. 2 - 1 - 3   2. 2 - 4 - 3 - 1   3. 2 - 3- 1 - 4

8 | 解答例） Good morning. My name is Fred. I'm from Australia. I'm twelve. I'm fine.
I'm not sleepy. Nice to meet you. など

UNIT 5

2 | 1. 緑(4) 赤(1) オレンジ(3) 青(2)   （音声） red blue orange green
2. 青(3) 白(4) 黒(1) ピンク(2)   （音声） black pink blue white

3 | 1. orange →オレンジ   2. white → 白   3. green →緑   4. red → 赤
5. black →黒   6. blue → 青   7. pink →ピンク

4 | (red) (blue) (pink) (green) (black) (orange) (white)

5 | 1. 算数   2. 社会   3. 英語   4. 理科   5. 音楽   6. P.E.
（音声）1. math   2. social studies   3. English   4. science   5. music   6. P.E.

6 | 1. 3 - 5 - 1 – 2 – 4 （音声）social studies music Japanese science math
2. 1 - 4 - 5 – 2 – 3 （音声）science English math P.E. Japanese

7 | 1. 理科   2. 音楽   3. 英語   4. 国語   5. 社会   6. 算数   7. 体育

11 | 1. Do you like social studies?   2. Do you like P.E.?   3. Do you like music?

14 | 1. I like   2. I don't like   3. Do you like / Yes I do / No I don't

UNIT6

2 | 1. 4 - 2 - 3 - 1   （音声）rugby baseball badminton tennis

2.　1 - 3 - 4 - 2　　（音声）soccer　volleyball　basketball　dodgeball

3.　1 - 3 - 4 – 2　　（音声）baseball　badminton　volleyball　basketball

3　
(5)　(7)　(1)　(6)
(4)　(3)　(8)　(2)

9　1.　Emily 🎾⚽　2.　Fred 🏏　3.　Jack ⚽🏉　4.　Alice 🏐
（音声）1.　I'm Emily.　I play tennis and soccer.
2.　I'm Fred.　I don't play rugby.　I play baseball.
3.　I'm Jack.　I play soccer.　I play rugby.
4.　I'm Alice.　I play dodgeball.　I don't play baseball.

10　解答例）I play tennis.　/ I don't play volleyball. など

12　1.　I play　　2.　I don't play　　3.　Do you play　/　Yes / I do　　No / I don't

UNIT 7

2　1.　3 - 2 - 1 - 4　　（音声）a pig　a dog　a cat　a goldfish
2.　3 - 1 - 4 - 2　　（音声）a panda　a monkey　a frog　a rabbit

3　1.　cat 🐱　2.　pig 🐷　3.　frog 🐸　4.　dog 🐶

4　1. ham – ster 🐹　2.　pan – da 🐼　3. rab – bit 🐰
4.　gold - fish 🐟　5. mon – key 🐵

5　1. p　2. a　3. n　4. d　5. a　　（動物のイラスト）panda

8　1. ○　2. ○　3. ×　4. ○　5. ×　6. ○
（音声）1.　I have a monkey.　2.　I have a hamster.　3.　I don't have a rabbit.
4.　I have a goldfish.　5.　I don't have a panda.　6.　I have a frog.

9　解答例）Do you have a dog?　Yes, I do. / Do you have a hamster?　No, I don't. など

12　1. 3 – 2 – 4 –1　　2. 4 – 1 – 3 –2

14 1. I have   2. I don't have   3. Do you have   Yes / I do   No / I don't

EXTRA(UNIT 5-UNIT 7)

1 Do you like baseball   / Yes   I do

4 1. have / don't have   2. play / like
   3. don't like / don't have   4. don't like / play

5 1. 2 - 1 - 3   2. 1 - 3 - 2 - 4   3. 3 - 1 - 2 - 4   4. 3 - 4 - 1 - 2   5. 1 - 4 - 3 - 2

6 1. C   2. D   3. A   4. B
   （音声）1. I don't have a dog. I have a cat.   2. I don't play tennis. I play baseball.
          3. I don't have a cat. I have a dog and a frog.
          4. I don't play baseball. I play tennis and soccer.

7 解答例) I play tennis.   I don't play soccer.   I like blue.   I don't like math.
          I have a rabbit.   I don't have a goldfish.   I am 10.   I am not tired.など

8   解答例) Hi! My name is Sachi. I'm eleven. I'm from Nara. I like soccer, too.
          I like English and math.

UNIT 8

2 1.   2.   3.   4.   5.   6.
  7.   8.

3 上段から run / ski / cook / jump / swim

4 1. 3 - 4 - 1 - 2   （音声）run   jump   ski   skate
  2. 3 - 1 - 4 - 2   （音声）swim   dance   sing   cook

5 1. リコーダーを吹く   2. 自転車に乗る   3. 高くジャンプする   4. 速く走る   5. じょうずに歌う

7 1. I can   2. I can   3. I can't   4. I can't   5. I can   6. I can't

9
  1. Kenta, can you ski? **No, I can't.** Can you run fast? **Yes, I can.**
     Can you play soccer? **No, I can't.**
  2. Ana, can you run fast? **No, I can't.** Can you ride a bike? **Yes, I can.**
     Can you sing well? **Yes, I can.**
  3. Emily, can you ski? **Yes, I can.** Can you ride a bike? **No, I can't.**
     Can you sing well? **No, I can't.**

10 解答例) I can swim.　I can play the recorder well.　I can't skate.　I can't run fast.
I like baseball.　I don't like dodgeball.　I have a dog.　I don't have a frog.

11 1.　4 - 2 - 1 - 3　　2.　3 - 1 - 4 - 2　　3.　2 - 1 - 4 - 3

13 1.　can play　2.　can't run　3.　Can you jump　　Yes / I can　No / I can't

UNIT 9

2 1. 1 – 3 – 4 – 2　　（音声）a pencil　a ruler　a notebook　a bag
　2. 1 – 2 – 3 – 4　　（音声）a pencil case　a pen　a book　a desk

3 1.　2.　3.　4.　5.
　6.　7.　8.　9.

6 1.　on　2.　under　3.　in　4.　on　5.　under　6.　on

8 1. 左に○　（音声）The bag is on the chair.　2．左に○　（音声）The ruler is in the bag.
　3. 右に○　（音声）The dog is on the desk.　4．右に○　（音声）The frog is under the dog.

9 1. ○　2. ×　3. ○　4. ○　5. ○　6. ×

10 解答例) 1. The cat is under the chair.　2. The pencil in the pencil case.
　3. The ruler is under the book. など

UNIT 10

2 1. a　2. a　3. an　4. a　5. an　6. a　7. a　8. an　9. a　10. a

4 1.　3 - 2 - 4 - 1　（音声）a strawberry　an orange　a banana　an apple
　2.　3 - 1 - 4 - 2　（音声）a carrot　a tomato　an onion　a radish
　3.　2 - 3 - 1 - 4　（音声）oranges　strawberries　bananas　melons
　4.　1 - 4 - 2 - 3　（音声）carrots　onions　radishes　potatoes

5 複数形　oranges→ tomatoes→ onions→ books→ strawberries→ apples

6 上段から m / e / l / o / n / s　　I like melons.

7 1. How many bananas do you have?　**I have three bananas.**
　2. How many strawberries do you have?　**I have ten strawberries.**
　3. How many potatoes do you have?　**I have five potatoes.**
　4. How many melons do you have?　**I have two melons.**
　5. How many onions do you have?　**I have seven onions.**

6. How many radishes do you have? **I have eight radishes.**

8 1. Kenta, how many pencils do you have? **I have seven pencils.**
    How many notebooks do you have? **I have five notebooks.**
    How many books do you have? **I have two books.**
    How many pens do you have? **I have three pens.**
   2. Fred, how many pencils do you have? **I have twelve pencils.**
    How many notebooks do you have? **I have eight notebooks.**
    How many books do you have? **I have eleven books.**
    How many pens do you have? **I have six pens.**
   3. Alice, how many pencils do you have? **I have nine pencils.**
    How many notebooks do you have? **I have seven notebooks.**
    How many books do you have? **I have three books.**
    How many pens do you have? **I have eleven pens.**

11 1. How / apples   2. many / two   3. How many / three

EXTRA (UNIT 8 -UNIT 10)

1 1. Under   2. Under   3. In   4. On   5. On

2 1. F   2. D   3. H   4. A   5. G

3 1. sing   2. play   3. ride   4. run   5. jump   6. cook

4 解答例）I can play dodgeball.   I can play the castanet.   I can cook *ramen*.
        I can't play baseball.   I can't play the piano.   I can't cook *okonomiyaki*.など

6 melons carrots   books   chairs   pencils   oranges   onions

7 上段から Do / don't / Do you / do / How many / five / two / three / Yes / ten

8 Fruits（果物）: a banana, an orange, an apple

   Vegetables（野菜）: an onion, a carrot, a potato

   Stationery（文ぼう具）: a pencil, a ruler, a notebook

9 pen bag chair desk notebook pencil ruler book
   banana apple melon potato onion carrot radish

10 結びつけるもの

    1. Mary - 4(four) - pencils   2. Tom - 10(ten) - notebooks   3. Jeff - 2(two) - rulers

    4. Alice - 7(seven) - bags

    （音声） 1．Hi, I'm Mary. I have four pencils.   2. Hello, I'm Tom. I have ten notebooks.

3. I'm Jeff. I have two rulers.　　　4. Hi, I'm Alice. I have seven bags.

11 | 1. ③　2. ⑤　3. ②　4. ①　5. ④

UNIT 11

2 | brother (4)　father (6)　grandma (5)　mother (2)　grandpa (3)　sister (1)
（音声）sister　mother　grandpa　brother　grandma　father

3 | （上から）kind – やさしい　big – 大きい　small – 小さい　tall – 背が高い
old – 年とっている　he – 彼　she – 彼女

4 | 1. a　2. e　3. o　4. i　5. a　6. a　7. a / i

5 | he : 　　　　she :

6 | 1. He　2. She　3. She　4. He　5. He　6. She

7 | 1. She　2. He　3. He　4. She　5. He

9 | 1. This is Hana.　She is my sister.　She is nine.
2. This is Fred.　He is my friend.　He is tall.
3. This is Meg.　She is my classmate.　She is twelve.
4. This is Ms. Brown.　She is my teacher.　She is from England.

10 | 1. is　2. is　3. am　4. are　5. is　6. is

11 | 解答例）Kenta is my friend.　Mr. Maeda is kind.

13 | 1. This is　2. She is　3. He is　4. is kind　5. is tall

UNIT 12

2 | 1. 2 - 4 - 3 - 1　（音声）a curtain　a bed　a table　a sofa
2. 2 - 1 - 4 - 3　（音声）a living room　a kitchen　a garden　a bathroom

3 | 1　 a kitchen　 a living room　 a garden　 a bathroom

2.　 a curtain　 a table　 a bed　 a sofa

4 | 1. e / d　2. o / a　3. a / e.　4. a / i

5　1. ③　2. ①　3. ④　4. ②　5. ⑤

6　1. by　2. in　3. under　4. behind

8　1. on　2. under　3. behind　4. by

11　START から順に Pam is under the tree. （もしくは Pam is by the tree.でも可）→ Pam is by the desk. →Pam is behind the chair.→ Pam is under the bed.→Pam is in the (plastic) bag.→Pam is behind the curtain. →

Pam is on the sofa. →Pam is on the dog.

UNIT 13

3　1. Sunday　2. Tuesday　3. Wednesday　4. Sunday　5. Saturday

4　1. 1 - 3 - 4 - 2　（音声）Monday　Thursday　Tuesday　Wednesday
　2. 4- 1 - 3 - 2　（音声）Friday　Sunday　Saturday　Thursday

5　火– Tuesday　水– Wednesday　木– Thursday　金– Friday　土– Saturday　日– Sunday

6　③ → ① → ② → ⑤ → ⑦ → ⑥ → ④

7　1. o / a　2. u / e　3. e / e　4. u / a　5. i / a　6. a / u　7. u / a

8　1. Tuesday　2. day / Friday　3. What day / Sunday　4. is it / Monday
　5. What / is / today / It's Saturday　6. What day is it today / It's Thursday

10　1. 5 - 1 - 3 - 2 - 4　（音声）It's two.　It's three.　It's six.　It's ten.　It's seven.
　2. 1 - 5 - 4 - 3 – 2　（音声）It's one.　It's twelve.　It's five.　It's four.　It's eight.

11　1. five　2. is it　3. What time /　two　4. 自由に書く

14　1. What time is it now　2. It's　3. five　4. It's three　5. It's (短針の数字) .

EXTRA(UNIT11 – UNIT13)

1　Sunday father bed kitchen garden table Thursday

2　Is she your friend?

3　I （am） / he, she, it (is) / you (are)

5 (START から順番に) It's one. → It's twelve. → It's two. → It's three. → It's eight.
→ It's four. → It's six. → It's nine. → It's eleven. → It's ten. → It's five. → It's twelve.

6 1. B   2. A   3. C   4. E   5. D

7 1. Thursday   2. ten   3. Pam   4. big   5. Three

8 1. 2 - 1 - 3   2. 3 - 1 - 2   3. 3 - 1 - 2 - 4   4. 1 - 3 - 2   5. 1 - 4 - 3 - 2

9 解答例) I am ten.   You are in the kitchen.   She is happy. など

11 1. ①○   ②○   ③×   ④×

    2. Sunday 午後 7 時 (時差は 9 時間、日本の方が 9 時間進んでいる)

UNIT14

2 1. 50 (fifty)   2. 13 (thirteen)   3. 18 (eighteen)   4. 7 (seven)
    5. 9 (nine)   6. 12 (twelve)   7. 21 (twenty-one)   8. 40 (forty)

4 1. 上から 3 つ目に✔   2. 上から 2 つ目に✔

5 1. 16   2. 20   3. 24   4. 33   5. 40   6. 13   7. 15   8. 18   9. 50

6 1. 28 → 50 → 33 → 47 → 18 → Kenta

    2. 25 → 15 →27 →47 →13 → Alice

    3. 10 →20 → 41→ 12 → 26→ Mr. Green

7 1. 15 (fifteen)   2. 13 (thirteen)   3. 17 (seventeen)   4. 22 (twenty-two)
    5. 29 (twenty-nine)   6. 28 (twenty-eight)   7. 46 (forty-six)   8. 30 (thirty)
    9. 14 (fourteen)   10. 39 (thirty-nine)

8 1. How old are you, Mike?   - I'm eighteen.
    2. How old are you, Ms. Sasaki?   - I'm twenty-four.
    3. How old are you, Mr. Green?   - I'm thirty-two.
    4. How old are you, Ms. Brown?   - I'm forty.
    5. How old are you, Mr. Ito?   - I'm fifty.

10 上から bananas - fourteen (14) / melons - twelve(12) / oranges - seventeen (17) /
    carrots - twenty-one (21) / potatoes - fifteen (15)

| 11 | 解答例) 1. Thirty (30) students. 2. Twelve (12) teachers. 3. Five (5) pencils. 4. Thirty-two (32) desks. 5. Fifty (50) bags.

UNIT 15

| 3 | 1. G 2. C 3. J 4. D 5. I 6. A 7. E 8. H 9. B 10. F

| 6 | Jump. 🧍 Sing. 🧍 Swim. 🏊 Play soccer. ⚽ Read. 📖

| 7 | 解答例) Don't walk. Don't turn right. など

| 9 | 1. Stop. 2. Turn left. 3. Go straight. 4. Don't write. 5. Don't swim. 6. Walk.

| 10 | 1. Write. 2. Don't run. 3. Sing. 4. Don't ride a bicycle.

UNIT 16

| 2 | 2 - 5 - 4 - 3 - 1 （音声）study eat breakfast get up go to bed eat dinner

| 3 | 1. D 2. C 3. B 4. A 5. E

| 4 | 解答例) 6:00 a.m. – 12:00 p.m. → 1, 3
12:00 p.m. – 6:00 p.m. → 4, 6
6:00 p.m. – 12:00 a.m. → 5, 6, 7, 8
12:00 a.m. – 6:00 a.m. → 2   など

| 8 | 1. 6:00 2. 6:30 3. 5:30

| 10 | 解答例) What time do you take a bath? / What time do you go to bed? など

| 11 | 1. What time do you get up, Alice? **I get up at seven.**
What time do you eat breakfast? **I eat breakfast at seven thirty.**
What time do you eat dinner? **I eat dinner at six.**
What time do you take a bath? **I take a bath at eight twenty.**
What time do you go to bed? **I go to bed at ten.**
2. What time do you get up, Jack? **I get up at six thirty.**
What time do you eat breakfast? **I eat breakfast at seven fifteen.**
What time do you eat dinner? **I eat dinner at six ten.**
What time do you take a bath? **I take a bath at seven forty.**
What time do you go to bed? **I go to bed at nine fifty.**
3. What time do you get up, Fred? **I get up at seven fifteen.**
What time do you eat breakfast? **I eat breakfast at seven forty.**
What time do you eat dinner? **I eat dinner at eight.**
What time do you take a bath? **I take a bath at nine thirty.**
What time do you go to bed? **I go to bed at eleven.**

13 1. 4 - 3 - 1 - 2   2. 2 - 1 - 3 - 4   3. 1 - 3 - 2 - 4   4. 2 - 3 - 1 - 4

EXTRA (UNIT14-UNIT16)

1 1. A   2. C   3. C

2 1. sixteen   2. twenty-four   3. forty   4. at three thirty   5. at two forty-five

3 (線でつなげる単語) 1. breakfast   2. a bath   3. TV   4. right   5. bed

4 1. at seven   2. at eight   3. at twelve   4. at four   5. at five

5 1. C   2. B   3. A   4. D

7 解答例) 「〜しなさい」Go to bed at eight.   Eat bananas.
「〜してはいけません」Don't go to school.   Don't take a bath.   Don't play soccer. など

8 ① C   ② D   ③ B   ④ E   ⑤ A

9 解答例) （上から）(I eat breakfast) at seven thirty.   (I eat lunch) at twelve.   (I go home)
at five.   (I eat dinner) at seven.   (I go to bed) at ten.など

UNIT 17

2 1. ⑥   2. ②   3. ①   4. ⑤   5. ④   6. ③

3 1. 2 - 3 - 1   (音声) a library   a park   an aquarium
2. 3 - 1 - 2   (音声) a swimming pool   a movie theater   a zoo

4 1. park   2. go / library   3. go to / zoo   4. want / go to / pool
5. want to go to / movie

5 5 - 4 - 1 - 2 - 3   (音声) France   Vietnam   Finland   Germany   South Africa

6 Korea ① / South Africa ④ / Canada ⑧ / China ③ /
France ⑥ / Vietnam ⑤ / Germany ② / India ⑦

7 1. i / a   2. i / a   3. a / e   4. e / a   5. i / a

9 1. go   2. do you / go   3. do you want / go   4. Where do you / to
5. Where / want to go

11 1. Where do you want to go?   **I want to go to the zoo.**
2. Where do you want to go?   **I want to go to the swimming pool.**

3. Where do you want to go? **I want to go to the aquarium.**
4. Where do you want to go? **I want to go to the movie theater.**

13　1.　2 - 4 - 1 -3　　2.　2 - 1 - 4 - 3　　3.　4 - 2 - 3 - 1

UNIT18

3　1月 January　2月 February　3月 March　4月 April　5月 May　6月 June

7月 July　8月 August　9月 September　10月 October　11月 November　12月 December

4　② → ⑥ → ① → ④ → ⑦ → ⑤ → ③

5　上段から **January　February　　March　　April　May　June　July　August**

　　September　　October　　November　　December

6　1.　1 - 4 - 2 - 3　　（音声）January　March　April　February

　　2.　4 - 1 - 2 - 3　　（音声）June　July　August　May

　　3.　4 - 2 - 3 – 1　　（音声）December　October　November　September

7　1.　February　2.　May　3.　September　4.　December　5.　March

　　6.　August　7.　January

9　上から順に　1st → first　5th→ fifth　8th→ eighth　2nd→ second

　　　　　10th→ tenth　3rd→ third　11th→ eleventh　12th→ twelfth

10　1.　rd　　2.　th　　3.　st　4.　th　5.　st　6.　th　7.　th　8.　nd　9.　th

　　10.　rd　　11.　nd　　12.　th

11　first→ second→ third→ fourth→ fifth→ sixth→ seventh→ eighth→ ninth→

　　tenth→ eleventh→ twelfth→ thirteenth→ fourteenth→ fifteenth

13　解答例）My birthday is October 8th. など

15　1. When is your birthday, Bill?　**My birthday is April 3rd.**

　　2. When is your birthday, Helen?　**My birthday is June 8th.**

　　3. When is your birthday, Mari?　**My birthday is November 17th.**

　　4. When is your birthday, Steve?　**My birthday is October 10th.**

　　5. When is your birthday, Peter?　**M birthday is July 12th.**

　　6. When is your birthday, Kate?　**My birthday is May 1st.**

EXTRA (UNIT 17-18)

1 1. z   2. p   3. l / y   4. m   5. m   6. m / p

2 1. A   2. C   3. E   4. B   5. D   6. F

3 解答例) First, I want to go to Hiroshima. I like *Hiroshimayaki*. など

4

（音声）I'm Alice. I want to go to the aquarium. I want to go to China, too.
Hi, I'm Fred. I want to go to the swimming pool in Vietnam.
Hello. I'm Emily. I like books. I want to go to the library. I want to go to Finland, too.
I'm Kenta. I want to go to the park in Australia.

5 BIRTHDAY

6 (first)(second)(third)(fourth)(fifth)(sixth)(seventh)(eighth)

7 1. February   2. 解答例) November, December, January, February など
   3. 解答例) July, August など   4. 解答例) July など   5. 解答例) September など
   6. January   7. June   8. November

8 1. Jack   2. Lucy   3. Bob   4. Mr. Green   5. Fred

フィンランド式
小学英語
ワークブック
初級

解答